MOSCOVIE CALM...

Czuieiow
Beriszagorod
Denjec R.
Daudro
Sariza
Tzornogar
Rne D'Ast...
NOGAI
BAUGH...
Ser...

NOGAIS
Sauts du Nieper
PETITE TARTARIE
Desert de Step
Volga Riu.
Astracan

Azak
Kuban Riu.
Belletecoi
CIRCASSIE
Bouches du V...
Cap de Suchater
Port de Munkischlan
Desert
AK Kariyah
Sibun

CRIMEE
Bachaze
Caita
Taman
Temruk
Besenada
CABARDINIE
M. Caucase
D'Challica Ostrow
TURKEMENS
Sellizure

de Carofqui
Cap de Circassie
MINGRELIE
IMIRETE
Rme DE
CARET
Riu de Terk
Terk
C. de Chatelet
Tzetlan ou Tzentzeni I.
MER CASPIENE
Korgange
CHOWAREZM
U

NOIRE
Port de Rif
d'Trisse
Trebisonde
Phasis
GURIEL
Akelzike
Teslis
DAGESTAN
Parku
Derbent, ou Porte de Fer
Niasabath
Scha
far stan

Calippe
Sinope
Os mange
Trebisonde
GIAGUAY
Gangea
Berde
Schiro
Chamaqui
VAN
Bakuje
Deserts
Sablonneux
Amberd

Amasie
Tocat
Sahabha
Athecala
Lac de
Kars
Echmelzin
IRAN
Erivan
Bilagan
Aras Riu
GOLFE DE GUILAN
Ferabath Escref ou Asharaf
Schamagol
ou Chigol
Noesa

Erzrom
Arzingan
Carputh
M. Palla
ARMENIE
TURCOMANS
Mus
Kellat
Arya
Van
Sophrani
Ardebil
Kesker
GHAN
Astrabath
Isfrani
Georgian ou Astabath
PAYS D'ASTABATH
CHORASAN
Sarachsch
ou Sarchas

ANATOLIE ASIATIQUE
M. Taurus
Ximael
Zeiad
Betlis
Albach
Tetouan
Salmas
Tauris
BRISTAN
Damogan
Bostan
Nischabur
Ferrior
Montagne ou l'on
trouve des Turquoises
Bueto
PAYS D'HERI
Herat ou Heri

Arots
Masjafarequin
Diarbekir
Zergue
Giousmarche
CURDISTAN
Senkegi
Salehieu
Ebher
Tahoran
CUMAS
Semnan
Chowan
Veremi
Desert Zuzen
Desert

Alexandrette
Antioch
Alepe
Ourfa
merdin
Nesbit
Mesul
Irbil
HAMadan
Saud
Kenghaser
Kom
Kaschan
M. Joilak Perfan
nomme autrefois
MONT TAURUS

CHYPRE
Taybe
Hanan
Rabam
Aruban
Raccaruinee
DIARBEK
Kerkesa
Rabba
Subercan
Gebbar
Slabna
Nohavand
Cranguie
Courmabad
Dehabad
Desert plein de Sel
Talkeare
Cors ou
Corea

Tripolis
Baruth
Damas
Oran
TURCOMANS
Ruines de
Thaamor ou
Palmyre
Anna
Hit ou est une
Source de Betume
Gedden
Hellan
Corbet
Cerryn
Ispahan
Iahad
Irabad
Iesd
Gustan
Desert de S. Esfaan
Kaiderm

Acre
Nazarorth
Zarka
Damna
Dans ces Deserts
on voit les Ruines de
plusieurs Villes
anciennes
Kerheen
Meschat Deem
Grand Palais
Deserte
LAURESTAN
Deserts
Giondisaru
Souftera
Laur
Komschach
Amnabad
larroia
Daru
Nadhea
Mastih

M. Kast ou il y a
Garnison
Maan Chateau et
Village habite
Lac de Rehemat
nomme par les Arabes
Al Bataveh
M. Rawzar
CHURSISTAN
Ahuaz ou
Haruze
Chilminar ou
Istachr ruine
RSISTAN
Kerman ou
petit Sirjan
Robin

Desert de l'Irac
Tschab Hasser ou il y a un
puits de bonne eau
IRAC
Balsord
Arjan
I. de Derghofan
Schiras
Passa
Darahgerd
KERMAN
Fahrag

ARABIE PETREE
Zathag Chateau ou
il y a Garnison
ARABIE DESERTE
Desert sans eau
ny habitation
Puits de bonne eau
Karghi
I. de Carek
I. de Rischer
Mt. de larron
Furg
Tafknie
Benaru
Bihry
Lar
Gubre
Bam
Tuberan
Giresft

ARABIE PETREE
Edu
Tirc
Meubelar
Montagnes de
l'Hijaz
Taboub ou Teboue Chateau
Taalabie
Desert sans eau
ny habitation
Ile de Chader
Cap Verd... Elfaine
Banc ou T. Cap Naban
I. Andu...
Queixome
GOLFE D'OR...
Isles de
I. Baherem

Madian nomme
par les Arabes
Mkar el Schouaib
ou Grote de Ietra
Al Mehadan
Chateau
Inhabite
Fadl
M. de Salma
Samnan
Tansia
Cap Verdel...
I. Lar.
Gouron
Bander
Cap Moxandar
Sohar
GOLFE D'OR...

Karzoka
Istambel ou
Estamboba
HAGIAR
PAYS DE NAGED
Merab
El Catif
Perles
El Ahsa
Benaru
MHA
Maskate
ROYAUME DE MASCATE

HIAGAR
PAYS DE THAMMUD
Vadia al Cora
Medine ou
Ville de Propheté
Iambo
Al Aala Chateau
et Village habite
Maadenalmoara
Chaibar
Arrags
Anize
Puits de mauvaise
eau
Salamia
NAGED habitez
par des Arabes
BAHREIN
Almadh
au Roy de Perse
Oman
Sohar

MER
Medine
Nabee
ETAT
HAROUDZ
ou
JEMAMA
Tima
Ismain ou
Hadrama
Cyriathain
Dania
Hajar ou
Hugar
Deserts
Eau et sans
bitu
Otion
Vodana
Masdate

ROYAUME DE MASCATE

A SILVER LEGEND

THE STORY OF THE MARIA THERESA THALER

A SILVER LEGEND

THE STORY OF THE MARIA THERESA THALER

CLARA SEMPLE

barzan

A Silver Legend

Copyright © Clara Semple 2005

The right of Clara Semple to be identified as the author of this work has been asserted by her in accordance with the Copyright, Designs and Patents Act of 1988.

Barzan Publishing Limited
Windrush Millennium Centre
Alexandra Road
Manchester M16 7WD
website: www.barzanpress.com

This edition published in association with
Stacey International
128 Kensington Church Street
London W8 4BH
Tel: +44 (0)207 221 7166
Fax: +44 (0)207 792 9288
E-mail: enquiries@stacey-international.co.uk
Website: www.stacey-international.co.uk

First published in Great Britain 2005
Published by Barzan Publishing Limited
Barzan Studies in Arabian Culture, No. 1

ISBN: 0-9549701-0-1

CIP Data: A catalogue record for this book
is available from the British Library

Design: Graham Edwards
Printing and binding: SNP Leefung, China

Photographic Credits:

All pictures by Clara Semple except for those which appear on the pages below. Illustrations are reproduced by courtesy and kind permission of the following:

Ash, P.J.: 105.
Ashmolean Museum: 31.
Austrian Mint: Title page,14, 28, 30, 39.
Bait al Zubair Museum, Muscat: 103, 109, 126.
Barclays Bank Archives: 146, 147.
Bjurström, Lars: 124.
Bodleian Library: 6, 62.
Bridgeman Art Library: frontispiece, vii, 9, 11, 13.
British Library: 136, 137.
British Museum: 2, 8, 12, 45, 50, 77, 82.
Fantich, Barry, *Saudi Aramco World*: coin front/back cover, v, 3, 5, 27t.
Fisher, Angela / Estell R., Photo Agency: 72, 130, 131.
Fr Bofelli: 98, 129.
Groom, Nigel: 76.
Hafner, Walter: 41, 44, 54, 64, 66, 69, 90t.
Harrigan, Peter: 101, 112.
Korenko, G.: 90.
Kunsthistorisches Museum, Vienna: Front Cover Portrait, 17, 18, 21.
Maréchaux, Pascal & Maria: vii, x, xi, xii, 106, 108, 151.
Mary Evans Picture Library: 55, 59, 63.
Ministry of Culture Sudan: 81, 83.
Museum of the Peasant, Bucharest: 92.
National Archives, Kew: 149.
Private collection of Sultan Ghalib Al Qu'aiti: map back cover, end papers, 65t.
Private source, Islamic Coins Group: 100.
Private source: 36
Private source: Niebuhr, C. *Travels in Arabia*: 52, 53.
Ransom, Marjorie: 118.
Rauch, H.D.,Vienna: 19, 24, 26, 27b, 33.
Royal Geographical Society: 78.
Royal Mint: 143, 145.
Schönbrunn Palace/Studio Johannes Wagner: 20.
Scully, Jil: 111, 114, 132.
Silverman, R. and Sobania, N.: vii, 4, 119.
Thesiger, Wilfred, Pitt Rivers Museum, Oxford: 85.
Völksbank Gunzburg: 38.
Weir, Shelagh: 117, 120, 123.
Wiener Bestattungsmuseum,Vienna: 23.

While every effort has been made to acknowledge copyright holders of images, if any individual or institution notices that they have not been included in the above list, would they please contact the publisher.

Frontispiece: Portrait of Empress Maria Theresa of Austria, Martin van Meytens (1695-1770).

The Maria Theresa Thaler 1780

An example of a modern restrike from the Austrian Mint 2004

Weight - 28.0668 grams   *Diameter* - 39.5 millimeters   *Silver content* - 833.3 parts per thousand

The titles in Latin on the obverse are
M•[ARIA] THERESIA•D•[EI] G•[RATIA] R•[ROMANORUM] IMP•[ERATRIX] HU•[NGARIAE]
BO•[HEMIA] REG•[INA]

'Maria Theresa by the Grace of God Empress of the Romans, Queen of Hungary and Bohemia'
The initials below the bust are those of the last names of the mintmaster, Tobias Schobel,
and warden, Joseph Faby, of the Gunzburg Mint in 1780.

The titles in Latin on the reverse are
[ARCHID•[UX] AUST•[RIAE] DUX• BURG•[UNDIAE] CO•[MES] TYR•[OLIS] 1780•X

'Archduchess of Austria, Duchess of Burgundy, Countess of Tyrol, 1780'
Following the date is the Saltire X in the form of the St Andrew's Cross.
The Imperial double-headed eagle with the arms of Austria at the centre is surrounded
by four quarters representing Hungary, Bohemia, Burgundy and Burgau.

The edge inscription reads
JUSTITIA ET CLEMENTIA

Acknowledgements

I owe a debt of gratitude to a number of people for their advice and encouragement during the writing of this book. Foremost amongst them is Walter Hafner of Vienna whose expertise in all matters concerning the Maria Theresa thaler he so willingly imparted. My particular thanks to Kerry Tattersall at the Vienna Mint who interrupted his hectic schedule to answer innumerable questions. I am most grateful to Adrien Tschoegl, Wharton Professor of Finance at the University of Wisconsin and to George Korenko of New York, and to Stefan Nebehay and Renate Meissner in Vienna, all of whom never failed to respond to my queries with patience and humour. My thanks to Helen Brown for sharing her knowledge of coins with such enthusiasm. I thank Dr Nick Mayhew and Dr Luke Treadwell at the Ashmolean Museum, Oxford and Dr Joe Cribb, at the British Museum, London for their forebearance in the face of my many enquiries. I would also like to register my thanks to Dr Clancy, Librarian and Curator of the Royal Mint Museum and to Graham Dyer as well as to the staff at the Barclays Bank Archives in Manchester, and to Johnson Matthey in London. The auction house H.D. Rauch in Vienna responded most kindly to my request for pictures as did Dick Doughty of Saudi Aramco World and Sara White and Saif Al Rawahi of the Bait al Zubair Museum in Oman. To John and Pamela Bunney in Vienna and Stuart and Sibella Laing in Oman my grateful thanks for their boundless hospitality in those countries.

I would like also to add my thanks to Professor Richard Pankhurst, Glencairn Balfour-Paul, Leila Ingrams, John Shipman, Sultan Ghalib Al Qu'aiti, Sarah Searight, Peter Adler, Jeremy Barnett, Hugh Leach, Shelagh Weir, Marjorie Ransom and Jehan Rejab, all of whom gave of their time and their ideas so generously. My heartfelt thanks to Graham Edwards for all his hard work on the design of this book.

Finally, I should like to thank Dr Mohammed al Rashid and Peter Harrigan of Barzan whose unwavering enthusiasm and support made this book possible.

Clara Semple
Oxford 2005

Contents

Foreword

A HABSBURG SURVIVOR

I t has long since ceased to be part of the Crown Currency of Austria and, perhaps, technically is no longer a coin. It has no fixed face value but it is a piece of silver of guaranteed weight and fineness. As such it is widely known and trusted.

The Times
London (1962)

A venerable Sudanese silversmith, who kept a small shop in the *souq* in Omdurman, gave me my first Maria Theresa thaler. Abd al-Karim came from a long line of silversmiths but at the time I came to know him his eyesight was failing and he had begun to accept fewer and fewer commissions. He spent much of his time reclining languidly on the floor of his shop, exerting himself only when required to weigh the bits and pieces of battered silver jewellery brought to him by the women of Omdurman. Most silversmiths were obliged to perform this task gratuitously and having one's old ornaments weighed before ordering a new piece such as a pair of armlets or anklets was a regular event.

Crouching beside Abd al-Karim I watched in alarm as his quivering hands placed a number of handsome Maria Theresa coins as counter-weights upon the flimsy scales. The whole apparatus shook precariously as he added various smaller weights, copper coins or glass beads to this edifice. It was like a conjurer's show: first the slow build-up of the act, followed by a brief dramatic climax when everything was suspended in time. Abruptly it was over and a rapid calculation was arrived at, so swiftly that it was impossible to know how it had been reached. For the rapt customers it was a moment of anticipation. If the amount declared did not meet their expectations, which it rarely did, the silver was tipped unceremoniously off the scales, the women gathered up their *thobes* and swept off towards the next silversmith's shop where the whole process was repeated. Acting as a measure of weight was, I realised, just one of several functions of this remarkable Austrian coin.

Before leaving Khartoum some years later I paid a last visit to Abd al-Karim. He rummaged deeply in a drawer, peering in, and with trembling hands stroked a number of coins before selecting a Maria Theresa thaler dated 1780, which he presented to me. Beneath the imperious effigy of the Empress he had engraved my name in Arabic, and declared that with the *abu riysh* to protect me I was assured a long and fruitful life. When questioned about the history of the coin he remained vague, jerking a sinewy arm behind his ear to indicate the past, *'qadeem, qadeem jiddan',* he declared, 'old, very old'.

It was only much later that I discovered my first thaler was not in fact minted in the year of its date but came from a mint in Birmingham sometime in 1949. I was not surprised, for by this time I had found myself unwittingly caught up in the story of a fascinating relic of a long gone Empire, and knew that the date 1780 on a thaler did not necessarily mean that it was minted in that year.

In the nineteen eighties and nineties my work took me further down the Nile valley to Egypt and then across the Red Sea to Arabia where, my passion being traditional silver jewellery, I came across Maria Theresa thalers in many unexpected places: in the Attareen *souq* of Alexandria where they lay gleaming in dusty showcases outshining the somewhat lacklustre Ottoman and French coins; or amidst the incense burners and sweet smelling *oudh* in the market place of Najran on the edge of the Empty Quarter. More intriguingly, I came across them in the dim recesses of the floating antique markets of Sarawak, where head-hunters were rumoured to offer them as blood

money. Each one of these enigmatic coins embodies a piece of history and, as it lay heavily in the palm of my hand, I was tempted to muse on its individual travels. Thus I was inspired to embark on the story of this silver legend.

I soon discovered that scholars and enthusiasts from a variety of disciplines such as numismatics, economics, history and ethnography have studied and written about this intriguing coin. I am indebted to these experts and the many travellers whose research and commentaries I have drawn upon in order to pull the separate strands of this story together.

C.S.

I

UNE FEMME D'ARGENT

A long the Blue Nile there is but one coin current – the Maria Theresa thaler – minted under the reign of the illustrious empress. In Austria it is long since out of circulation but because of a continuing demand in Abyssinia and Sudan it is still coined by private persons of the mint in Vienna.

Juan Maria Schuver
Travels in North East Africa 1880-1883

By the time Juan Maria Schuver wrote these words, the Habsburg Empress Maria Theresa had been dead for exactly one hundred years. Her magnificent silver thaler lived on, however, circulating ever more widely in distant lands, acquiring near mythological status in remote sultanates and desert strongholds across Africa, Arabia and well beyond: places where the minting of coinage was little known. The next hundred years would see these astonishing coins continue on their passage: a river of silver

---

Previous pages:
A Yemeni shepherdess wearing a girdle of thalers

Left:
A woman from the Jabal Milhan in northern Yemen wearing traditional festive costume.

flowing out of Europe across the Mediterranean to Egypt and into the Red Sea and North and East Africa. They were exchanged for coffee from Yemen, slaves from Ethiopia and Sudan, and a profusion of exotic wares from the East.

To follow the migration of the Austrian thaler over its two-hundred-year odyssey is to discover fascinating aspects of diverse and little-known lands. Commerce was its *raison d'être,* but along the way it became embroiled in intrigues of many kinds. Ransoms and blood money were paid in Maria Theresa thalers; clandestine missions had recourse to them, and they played a crucial role in the Horn of Africa during the Second World War. Speculators built trading empires with the profits of their trade when the price of silver rose, and millions were hoarded in subterranean galleries by despotic rulers. They were regularly buried underground for safe-

1

Territoire de Circulation

DU

THALER de MARIE-THÉRÈSE

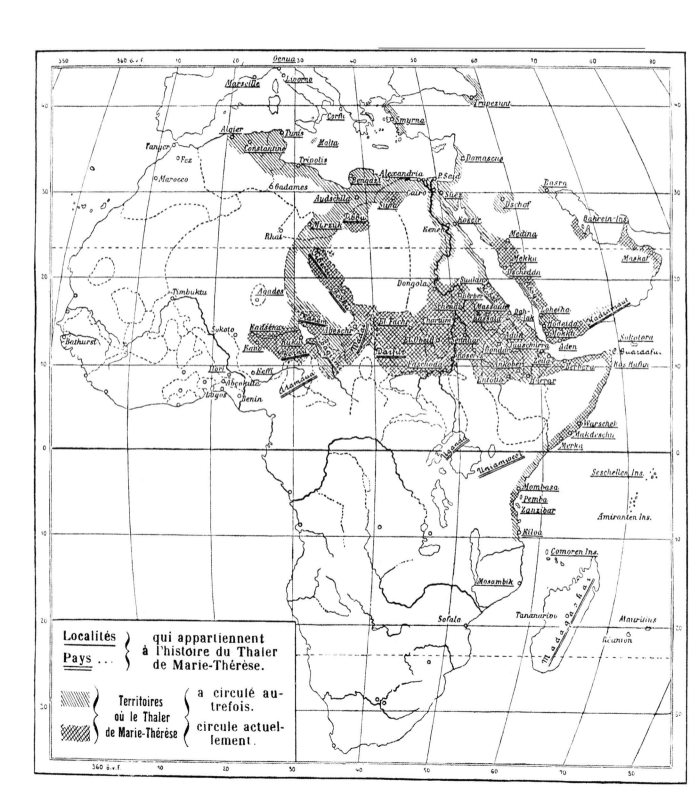

Left:
A map showing the circulation of the Maria Theresa thaler published by C.Peez and J. Raudnitz in Vienna, 1898.

Below:
The obverse and the reverse of the Maria Theresa thaler, 1780. Austrian Mint 2003.

keeping, or to hide them from the depredations of robbers and intrusive tax collectors.

Levantine merchants of the seventeenth and eighteenth centuries understood the merits of a reliable silver coin and favoured payment *in specie* over barter and exchange. The Maria Theresa thaler was but one of several large silver coins to be traded in the Levant, including the Dutch lion dollar and the Ottoman *mejidi*. The Spanish dollar or real also enjoyed great popularity in parts of Africa and Arabia from the sixteenth to the nineteenth century, when it was gradually superseded by the more dependable Austrian coin.

The Empress died in 1780, and in the normal course of events her coinage would have simply been withdrawn from circulation or demonetised. However, such was the demand for the lustrous silver thaler abroad that her son, the Emperor Joseph II, agreed that it should be re-struck with the date frozen at 1780. Thus the Maria Theresa thaler acquired the status of a trade coin.

How and why this particular Habsburg coin gained such pre-eminence over all others throughout such an extensive area and for such a long time, is a question frequently posed and one to which there is no simple answer. Howland Wood writing in *The Coin Collectors Journal* in 1936, observed that, 'the tenacity with which this coin has held its own, meeting all rivals, may be called one of the wonders of numismatics and seems almost to refute common sense as it is unredeemable except for bullion.' In fact the Maria Theresa thaler's considerable intrinsic value had always been one of its most powerful

Left:
A young girl from Aleyu Amba in Ethiopia wearing a necklace of beads interspersed with Maria Theresa thalers.

attributes. Nowadays coins are simply tokens issued by a government and have little intrinsic value, but in the past coins made from silver or gold were valued for their metal content and were traded like any other commodity. In his *Discourse upon Coins* printed in 1588, Bernardo Davanzati explained that commodity money had its value from the supply and demand for bullion and was valued everywhere. At the same time, however, the value could fall swiftly depending on a variety of factors such as scarcity, supply and demand, or the price of silver and gold.

The extraordinary popularity of the Maria Theresa thaler was the result of a careful fostering of trust by both the merchants of the Levant and the Austrian authorities who, with consummate care, promoted it in their trade

with the Middle East. They did this by ensuring that the silver content remained constant, as any debasement, however minor, would deprive it of its carefully cultivated reputation. Furthermore, all parties tried to ensure that the coin remained absolutely identical in every respect to the original 1780 version. Any change was viewed with suspicion. When variations in the minting did creep in, this led to confusion, distrust, and even rejection.

Considered by many to be the most beautiful coin in the world, the high silver content of the thaler imparts an exceptional lustre. The imposing profile of the Queen-Empress surrounded by her titles in Latin is particularly finely engraved, as is the reverse with the elaborate Imperial insignia of eagle and crowns. Because of its intricate detail it has long been held to be impossible to counterfeit. One particular feature set the Maria Theresa thaler apart from other coins: its embossed edge, which bears the motto of the Empress, *Justitia et Clementia*. This acted as a deterrent against 'clipping,' a fraudulent practice whereby snippets of silver were shaved off the edges of silver and gold coins. Few other coins enjoyed this particular advantage and over the years this was to prove one of its greatest assets.

The Maria Theresa thaler developed a symbiotic alliance with the traditional silver jewellery of Arabia and Eastern Africa. Silversmiths relied on these coins for their high silver content as there were few alternative sources of silver. Millions of thalers found their way into crucibles to be melted down. There is little doubt that the coin facilitated and inspired a vibrant tradition of jewellery in many countries where it circulated. Moreover the coin itself was a coveted component in the necklaces, belts and headdresses worn by women who believed it to have protective or amuletic properties. Thalers also formed a vital part of dowry payments at a time of betrothal and were easily converted into the wedding jewellery that formed an indispensable part of the bridewealth in many societies.

It was not until the early years of the twentieth century that the Maria Theresa thaler gradually gave way to the national currencies being adopted by newly created states in Arabia and Africa. For years there had been attempts to dislodge it in some countries but it was famously tenacious. First the Ottomans and then other colonial powers issued decrees and passed draconian laws in an effort to get rid of it. It lingered on for decades in gradually diminishing quantities. As a coin of trade, its end finally came with the universal adoption of fiduciary money, that is, money whose value depends on trust rather than on its intrinsic value.

Although sometimes known as the coin without a country, the Maria Theresa thaler found a home in many countries. As an international currency it was traded seamlessly across borders, like the Euro of today. Although the 'much travelled lady' has long since retired, it continues to be produced in the Vienna Mint, albeit in far smaller quantities. To date it is estimated that nearly four hundred million thalers have been minted since they were first struck in 1741.

Below:
The embossed edge inscription with part of the Latin motto JUSTITIA ET CLEMENTIA.

Der ſchacht zwar/ſo er biß zum ſtollen kompt/ſo ſthet die ſach woll/vñ nem
mē die heuwer ſampt anderē taglöner die arbeit willig auff ſich/ſo er aber nicht
ſo tieff iſt/ſo müß man die andere ſeitē/oder alle beide grabē vñ außhauwē/auß
welcher hauwūg ð gwerck oder ſteiger die gäng vñ klüſſt ð grübē erkēt/welche
eintweders mitt dē haup1gang/ſo in die tieffe fellt/voñ welchē ich allhie rede/
zũſamen fallen/oder ſie creutzweiß oð flach zerteilendt/vñ ſonderlich von ð ma

A VALLEY OF SILVER

The almighty dollar. That great object of universal devotion throughout our land.

Washington Irving

A party of noblemen out hunting in the valley of St Joachimsthal in Bohemia took shelter in some caves from a sudden storm. This chance happening in the sixteenth century led to the discovery of deposits of silver ore in unprecedented quantities. Count Stephen von Schlick, the fortunate landowner and beneficiary of this unexpected treasure lost no time in seeking permission to strike coins in his name.

During the next two centuries prodigious

___

Left:

A woodcut from Agricola's 'De Re Metallica', a sixteenth century discourse on mining. The illustration shows the primitive and dangerous nature of mining techniques in the sixteenth century. Large new discoveries of silver throughout Europe at that time brought about an urgent need for new and improved machinery such as pumping equipment to allow miners to penetrate deeper underground.

quantities of silver were extracted from the mines of this Bohemian valley and from it handsome coins were made. They became known as *St Joachimsthalers*. This cumbersome name was soon abbreviated to thaler, from 'thal' or 'tal', the German word for valley. Dutch traders referred to them as *dalers*, in Swedish they were known as *daalders*, and in English, dollar.

The thaler was not the first large silver coin of its kind. It had a well-known antecedent, the *guldiner* or *guldengroschen*, which circulated throughout Europe and beyond in the fifteenth and sixteenth centuries. These *guldengroschen* were minted privately by the rulers of various princely fiefdoms, ducal states, and archbishoprics in Europe. The large surfaces of these coins allowed the engraver plenty of scope to express his artistic talents, and the elaborate images which resulted were designed to impress. These so-called 'show thalers' were often struck to commemorate a special event, such as a victory in battle or the death of a ruler.

Above left:
The St Joachimsthaler of Count Stephen von Schlick, named after the valley of St Joachim in present day Czech Republic, where large quantities of silver were mined in the sixteenth century. The word 'thaler' became a generic name for a large silver coin weighing about an ounce or 28 grams.

Below left:
A handsome four thaler coin of 1662, commissioned by the Duke of Brunswick-Lüneburg in celebration of the wealth derived from his silver mines.

Influenced by the style of Renaissance medals, portraits on coins became increasingly realistic. Florid effigies of noblemen displayed intricately engraved wigs and ruffs. Bishops wore sumptuous robes, and knights were clad in elaborate armour, seated astride richly caparisoned chargers, pennants aloft. Encircling these effigies were titles and legends in ornate Latin script that were so lengthy they had to be abbreviated.

Many of these distinctive silver coins found their way abroad in lucrative foreign trade. Examples of coins depicting swashbuckling archdukes and moustachioed emperors can occasionally be found in museum showcases in Arabia and East Africa, taken to those countries by European traders in the seventeenth century. Sometimes one comes to light in a *souq*, like the early Habsburg thaler of Joseph I dated 1706, discovered gathering dust in a silversmith's shop in the hinterland of the Yemen.

One of the most widely circulating trade coins dating from the sixteenth century – and the only serious rival to the Maria Theresa thaler – was the Spanish real. This coin was the result of an edict of 1497 in which King Ferdinand and Queen Isabella of Spain ordained 'that there shall be struck silver money to be called *reale*.' Reals and their successors minted in the Spanish colonies of South America were to become the most renowned currency of their age, and circulated even more widely than the Maria

Above:

The Aztec chieftain, Maxixcatzin, presents a bouquet of roses and other gifts to Hernando Cortes (1485-1547) as tokens of welcome, illustration from an 1892 facsimile of a Mexican Indian picture history 'Lienzo de Tlaxcala' of c.1550.

Theresa thaler. The name real reflects the coin's royal origins and lives on to this day as the riyal, the currency of several Arab countries. The first reals came in different denominations such as the eight-real or the fifty-real, but by far the best known was the 'piece of eight'. The earliest reals were crudely made, of uneven shape, and were frequently cut into eight pieces, which is how they earned their name. As the Spanish coin became more widespread it took on other names such as the peso and the dollar.

Following the Spanish conquest of Mexico by Cortes in 1518 and Pizarro's success in Peru six years later, fabulous amounts of silver became available to the colonists. The silver mountain of Potosi (now in Bolivia) was discovered in 1545 and yielded enormous quantities of the precious metal over the following centuries.

The Aztecs customarily wore their silver as ornaments and used cocoa beans for trading purposes, but their new Spanish rulers soon introduced them to the advantages of silver currency. Silver reals, depicting the profile of the Habsburg Emperor Charles V, (Charles I of Spain), were first minted in Mexico in 1536. Known as 'pillar dollars,' they displayed on the reverse side two columns capped with crowns. These represented the Pillars of Hercules, the mythical columns Hercules is reputed to have erected on the rocky outcrops on the opposite sides of the Straits of Gibraltar and which were entwined with the inscription *'ne plus ultra'*, alluding to the outer limits of the known world. On the Spanish coin the ribbon is shown wound around the columns and bears the legend *'plus ultra'*, the motto adopted by Charles V in celebration of the Spanish conquests in the New World, and which is still inscribed on the Spanish Royal Coat of Arms.

'Pieces of eight' or 'pillar dollars' were dominant for years across the world. Familiar in every port, they were particularly popular in the Far East as well as in many parts of Africa and Arabia. However, they never achieved the reputation for reliability which made the Maria Theresa thaler endure for so long. In the 1650s 'a scandalous falsification' occurred when silver coins from the Peruvian mints were debased, and during the following hundred and fifty years the silver content of the Spanish dollar continued to fall. By the middle of the nineteenth century, following Spain's loss of its possessions in the Americas, the Spanish coin began to be superseded by the Maria Theresa thaler in Arabia and Africa. 'The Spanish Government has refused to perpetuate its Pillar dollar, which at one time was so great a favourite in the East', noted Sir Richard Burton in 1850 during his pilgrimage to Makkah and al-Madinah. The Mexican dollar took its place, but despite being popular in the Far East it was no match for the Maria Theresa thaler in those countries where the Austrian coin had become entrenched.

Above:
A Spanish 'pillar dollar'. The columns each with a ribbon wound around them are believed to be the origin of the dollar sign. The columns were sometimes confused with cannons and were known in Arabic as abu midfa *(father of the cannon).*

Much of this silver coinage was shipped back to Spain to pay for the Habsburg wars, while some of it was transported by the galleons of the Spanish treasure fleet across the Indian Ocean to the Philippines, whence it was traded on to China in exchange for spices, tea, and rare porcelain. The Chinese appetite for silver was insatiable, much to the dismay of their European trading partners, who were obliged to pay in hard cash when they would have preferred to barter for their goods.

Spanish dollars circulated throughout South America and eventually found their way north where they were used by British colonists who,

One of the earliest literary references to dollars comes in *Macbeth*, even though the dollar was never an English currency:

'Nor would we deign him burial of his men
Till he disbursed, at Saint Colme's Inch,
Ten thousand dollars to our general use.'
Macbeth (1.ii.62)

Furthermore, dollars are mentioned only in those plays of Shakespeare written during the reign of James I, who, as James VI of Scotland, was known to have taken an interest in coinage and struck the so-called 'thistle dollar' using the rich deposits of silver from the mines near Stirling in Scotland. In *King Lear* we find a characteristic Shakespearian punning play on the words 'dollar' and 'dolour', as the Fool warns Lear: *'thou shalt have as many dolours for thy daughters as thou canst tell in a year.'*
King Lear (II.iv.52)

even though they made their calculations in pounds and shillings, used the Spanish coins for their day-to-day transactions.

For most people the dollar is inextricably associated with the United States of America. After the American War of Independence it was Thomas Jefferson who, in 1785, first proposed that it should be adopted as the currency of the country, for he considered it to

be 'the most familiar of all to the minds of the people.' Jefferson was actually referring to the Spanish real or dollar which had circulated throughout the Americas from the time that it was first minted after the Spanish conquest in the early sixteenth century.

Jefferson worked hard to bring order to a monetary system which was in chaos, and he came up with the idea of using the decimal

Left:
The first American silver dollar, known as the Liberty Dollar, was struck in 1792. The image on the obverse of the coin expressed the freedom of the newly independent states of America.

Below left:
The earliest known coinage in the Western world was made by the Lydians who used electrum, an alloy of silver and gold, which occurred naturally in Asia Minor. The metal was cast into irregular plump discs and stamped with a symbol or a mark, signifying the weight or provenance.

Below right:
The Athenian owl coin, a popular and long-lived currency from the sixth century BC.

unit as a basis for monies and weights. In 1792 the Congress of the Confederation of the United States decreed that the official coinage should be the dollar. It became a potent symbol of freedom and has maintained its status as one of the pre-eminent currencies in the world.

Nearly 2,000 years before Shakespeare, Herodotus wrote that 'The Lydians in Asia Minor under King Croesus were the first nation to use silver and gold coins to buy and sell goods.' Until then trade had been conducted by barter or exchange of goods, but with the advent of a medium such as a coin with a fixed value, the

opportunities for trading were clearly improved.

More sophisticated were the famous silver 'owl' coins of Athens dating from the sixth century BC. Stamped with the endearing image of an owl, they were made in great quantities throughout Greece over a considerable period of time, and were traded as far afield as Egypt and Afghanistan. Much of their success was due to the fact that the design remained unchanged, and like the Maria Theresa thalers, they survived because of their familiarity. Both coins were also much imitated, a testimony to their enduring popularity.

Below:
A view of the silver mountain of Potosi by Martin Englebrecht (1684-1756).

Maria Theresia, von Gottes Gnaden römische Kaiserin, Wittib, Königinn zu Hungarn, Böheim, Dalmatien, Croatien, Slavonien etc., Erzherzoginn zu Österreich, Herzoginn zu Burgund, zu Steyer, zu Kärnten und zu Krain, Großfürstinn zu Siebenbürgen, Markgräfinn zu Mähren, Herzoginn zu Braband, zu Limburg, zu Luxenburg und zu Geldern, zu Würtenberg, zu Ober- und Niederschlesien, zu Mayland, zu Mantua, zu Parma, zu Placenz und Quastalla, Fürstinn zu Schwaben, gefürstete Gräfinn zu Habsburg, zu Flandern, zu Tirol, zu Hennegau, zu Kiburg, zu Görz und Gradisca, Markgräfinn des Heiligen Römischen Reichs zu Burgau, zu Ober- und Nieder Lausitz, Gräfinn zu Namur, Frau auf der Windischen Mark und zu Mecheln etc. verwittible Herzoginn zu Lotharingen und Baar, Großherzoginn zu Toskana etc.

III

THE QUEEN WHO COINED A LEGEND

*N*ever did any princess ascend a throne under circumstances of greater peril or which demanded more fortitude, energy and personal resolution.

Sir William Wraxall

Memoirs of the Courts of Berlin, Dresden, Warsaw and Vienna (1806)

Maria Theresa's accession to the Habsburg throne in 1740 was sudden and dramatic. Her father Charles VI, Holy Roman Emperor, King of Hungary and Bohemia, Archduke of Austria, Duke of Tyrol, Styria, and Carinthia, and bearer of many further illustrious titles, died unexpectedly, leaving his 23-year-old daughter to succeed him. Although she had felt from an early age that she was destined to inherit the throne, the task of ruling over the vast collection of disparate lands and nationalities which comprised the Habsburg Empire was a formidable one, and there were many who

thought that the inexperienced princess would find the undertaking beyond her, particularly as her father had done little to prepare her for high office, nor had he left much in the treasury. To add to her difficulties, within a month of her new rule, she had to face not only the threat of invasion by King Frederick II of Prussia, but also a challenge to her Habsburg inheritance from her cousin, the Elector Charles Albert of Bavaria. No wonder Maria Theresa lamented the inauspicious circumstances of her accession. It was a measure of her strength of character and fortitude, combined with a practical and clear mind, that she was able to achieve peace and stability during her forty-year reign, and to institute far-reaching social and political reforms.

Born on May 13, 1717 to the Emperor

Left:
The Habsburg crest with all Maria Theresa's titles below.

Charles and his wife, the beautiful Elizabeth Christina of Brunswick-Wolfenbuttel, Maria Theresa and her younger sister enjoyed an idyllic, carefree childhood in the sprawling Hofburg Palace in Vienna. Although the Emperor appeared dour and serious in public, he liked nothing better than to organise costly theatrical extravaganzas, operas, and concerts which usually took place in the fairytale gardens of the Favorita Palace, on a hillside beyond the city walls. Maria Theresa adored dancing, and had an exceptionally fine singing voice. Her father never stopped hoping that he might yet produce a male heir and made little effort to instruct Maria Theresa in affairs of state. However, in her interest, he took great pains to formulate the famous imperial edict known as the Pragmatic Sanction of 1713, which he hoped would guarantee the indissolubility of the Habsburg lands and at the same time sanction the female succession in the event of there being no male heir.

Tall, with deep blue eyes and an abundance of blonde hair, the youthful and vivacious Archduchess grew into a considerable beauty. She was described by Sir Thomas Robinson, the British Ambassador to Vienna, as being 'very beautiful, her person formed to wear a crown, with a winning and animated face, a noble figure, and fascinating manners.' There were many contenders for her hand in marriage among the nobility of Europe, but for Maria Theresa there was only ever one man, her beloved Francis Stephen, Duke of Lorraine, whom she had known and adored since she was six years old. They were married in 1738, and despite his many infidelities she loved him with a passion that endured until his death. As the price for French recognition of the Pragmatic

Sanction, he was obliged to relinquish his title and lands in Lorraine in return for an inheritance to the Dukedom of Tuscany on the death of the last ruler of the house of Medici. Although Francis had little interest in politics, he was astute in business matters and gave useful advice on the rehabilitation of the state finances, while amassing a huge private fortune.

The royal couple enjoyed many years of conjugal happiness, producing 16 children in the first 19 years of marriage, three of whom died in infancy and three in early youth. By all accounts the Hofburg Palace was more like a nursery than a royal residence. Endowed with stamina, Maria Theresa combined her constitutional duties with the demands of her growing family. Court life was relaxed and informal, with the Emperor and Empress devoting a considerable amount of time to bringing up their children. They all excelled at music, dancing, acting and singing and the palace reverberated with their youthful talents.

Known as 'Europe's mother-in-law', Maria Theresa was ruthless in pursuing politically advantageous marriages for her children, most notably that of fourteen year-old Maria Antonia – Marie Antoinette as she was to become – to the future King of France, Louis XVI. She maintained her maternal control from a distance, writing numerous letters to her children long after they had married and left home. Marie-Antoinette, for instance, received a

constant flow of instructions from her mother regarding her behaviour at the French court.

Maria Theresa faced the first challenge to her inheritance under the Pragmatic Sanction at the start of her rule in 1740. The newly-crowned Frederick II of Prussia marched swiftly into Silesia with his large and well-trained army. Devastated, Maria Theresa was determined to fight for her inheritance whatever the consequences, and there followed years of

Above:
The Imperial couple surrounded by their family. Maria Theresa was portrayed as a powerful mother figure. She was described as 'heroically fertile' as she bore sixteen children, three of whom died in infancy. Her youngest daughter was Marie Antoinette, who became Queen of France.

Opposite:
Gold 5 ducat coin issued for the coronation of Maria Theresa as Queen of Bohemia in 1743.

invasion and counter-invasion as she struggled to keep the Habsburg lands intact. Finally forced to make concessions, she relinquished Silesia to the Prussian king. It was an embittering experience but worse was to come. The Pragmatic Sanction was again threatened when her cousin by marriage, Charles Albert, Elector of Bavaria, invaded Upper Austria in 1741, and took the city of Prague and with it the crown of Bohemia. It was at this critical point in the War of the Austrian Succession that Maria Theresa showed she was a force to be reckoned with. Against the advice of her elderly courtiers, she made an impassioned appeal to her Hungarian subjects to support her. Pale and vulnerable, her golden hair streaming onto her shoulders, she stood before a throng of Hungarian nobles and, addressing them in Latin, pledged her trust and utmost cooperation with Hungary at all times in the future. Charmed by her extreme youth, her future subjects responded with wild adulation. The fiery support of the Hungarian people helped to drive the French, Prussian and Bavarian armies out of Prague and Bohemia.

Maria Theresa became Empress when her husband was elected Holy Roman Emperor after the death of Charles VII in 1745, who, as Charles Albert, Elector of Bavaria, had seized the Imperial crown with the collusion of the French. Maria Theresa used all her influence to have her husband elected Holy Roman Emperor, an ancient and illustrious title, but one that carried little real power. She did not attend his coronation in Frankfurt as it is said that she did not wish to upstage him. In September 1741, Maria Theresa was crowned Queen of Hungary in a lavish ceremony which culminated in a dramatic finale when, according to ancient custom, the youthful archduchess, dressed in coronation regalia and wielding a sword, rode up onto an artificial mound astride a charger.

Maria Theresa began a series of far-reaching social and institutional reforms for which she became famous. Realising that the army was in urgent need of modernization and expansion, she set up several military academies to improve the training of the standing army. Financial reforms were her next priority. She introduced a taxation system in which the privileges of the rich landowning nobility were curtailed, and by the end of her reign she had managed to double the state revenues. Much-needed reforms of the civil service and other state institutions, such as the judiciary, followed. An effective education system was introduced with the aim of establishing secondary schools in all the major towns, and the reforms instituted for the welfare of the peasants were rightly celebrated.

These reforms were put in place through the agency of handpicked advisors such as Count Haugwitz, the brilliant diplomat Prince Kaunitz, and Gerhard von Swieten, Maria Theresa's personal physician, who advised on medical reforms and the new education system. An

Left:
An eighteenth century engraving of the young Queen by Elias Ridinger.

Below:
The Palace of Schönbrunn painted by Canaletto in the mid eighteenth century. This was Maria Theresa's favourite residence, a former hunting lodge which, under her supervision, was extended and improved.

indefatigable worker, the Empress was endowed with almost superhuman energy that allowed her to spring back into the saddle of official duties during the short spells between her many pregnancies. Within hours of childbirth she was signing state papers and penning copious memoranda in her notoriously untidy hand. She was often to be seen taking papers with her in a little box tied to her waist as she walked in the gardens of Schönbrunn Palace.

It was in the middle years of her reign that Maria Theresa undertook the ambitious project of transforming Fisher von Erlach's original hunting lodge into the grandeur of the Schönbrunn Palace which stands today as a reminder of her illustrious reign. Under her supervision and with the help of the Italian architect Nicolaus Pacassi, the lodge was turned into a magnificent example of Austrian Rococo,

a style she much admired. Schönbrunn soon became the centre of court life, replacing the Hofburg in central Vienna as her preferred home. Here her numerous children could relish the light airy space after the relative gloom of the Hofburg. The palace gave onto gardens not unlike those of Versailles, with a series of vistas culminating in elaborate fountains, temples and pavilions. The Emperor Francis busied himself with creating a zoological garden in the palace grounds, with an exotic palm house.

Both the Emperor and Empress loved spectacular outdoor entertainments of opera or fireworks, the more elaborate the better. Two theatres were in constant use and the court poet Metastasio produced librettos as well as poems. Because music was an integral part of life at the court, the Schönbrunn Palace was a magnet for talent. Both Glück and Haydn composed and played for the royal couple, and as a small boy Mozart was taken to meet the Empress. However, she was more a patron of entertainers than of serious musicians according to one of her biographers, Edward Crankshaw, and when years later the struggling Mozart applied for a job with her son Ferdinand, she firmly advised against it, failing completely to perceive the unique genius of the young prodigy.

The year 1753 saw the 'Reversal of the Alliances', for Austria and France were now allied against England and Prussia. Maria Theresa's reformed army inflicted defeat on the Prussians, though Silesia was lost forever. Despite this Maria Theresa had reason to be satisfied as, by 1765, after an exhausting two decades, she had succeeded in consolidating much of her inheritance, and in spite of the loss of Silesia, she had worsted her bitter enemy Frederick II. But, about to face the worst crisis of her life, she had

Right:
The elaborate sarcophagus containing the remains of the Emperor and Empress which lies in the vaults of the Capuchin Church in Vienna. From the book TAPHOGRAPHIA PRINCIPUM AUSTRIAE ... QUOD EST MONUMENTORUM AUG, DOMUS AUSTRIAIACAE. TOMUS IV. & ULTIMUS, MARTINUS GERBERTUS, EIUSDEM CONGREGATIONIS ABBAS, MDCCLXXII (1772), Wiener Bestarrungsmuseum

no time to enjoy victory. She was utterly bereft when her beloved husband collapsed and died quite suddenly. Her life changed forever, although she continued to rule with her son Joseph II as co-regent. It was never an easy alliance for they were of such opposite temperaments, and she found him difficult and overbearing.

The Empress in widowhood was a sad figure, draped in black, her glorious hair covered in a simple widow's cap. Her husband's remains were interred in a massive bronze sarcophagus elaborately carved in the rococo style so beloved by her, which depicts the couple in an everlasting embrace. Fifteen years were to pass before the body of the Empress took its place beside her husband, a sad passage of time during which her legendary energy slowly diminished. Growing increasingly corpulent and crippled with arthritis, she nevertheless remained devoted to her regal duties and continued to care passionately for her subjects' welfare.

Maria Theresa passed away peacefully sitting at work in a chair, still occupied with documents and letters of state and refusing to sleep for, with her inimitable courage, she wished to 'see death coming'. She died on November 29, 1780.

Tab. LXXXVII.

MONVMENTI SEPVLCRALIS FRANCISCI ET MAR. THERESIAE AVGG.
APVD P.P. CAPVCCINOS IN VRBE VIENNENS. PARS ORIENTALIS.

A. Salomone Kleiner delin. et aeri incisa. 1759. Mon. Aust. T. IV. P. II.   SS. SS.

IV

IMPERIAL THALER

The first purpose of coins is to serve as a social commodity – the hard cash designed for the practical, everyday business of hand-to-hand exchange. Accordingly therefore, as they have been issued at a time when religion, commerce, wars, politics have been uppermost in national consciousness, they have at most periods reflected the spirit of their time.

C.H.V. Sutherland
Art in Coinage (1955)

The appearance in 1741 of the profile of a strikingly beautiful young woman on the coinage of the Austrian Empire provided a welcome change from the long history of fiercely masculine Habsburg rulers with their craggy profiles, prominent underlips and monstrous wigs. Maria Theresa was the first female to inherit the Habsburg throne, and the coin engravers and medallists rose magnificently to the challenge. Singularly rich and diverse varieties of denominations in gold and silver

were struck: thalers, half-thalers, quarter-thalers, ducats, gulden and kreuzers. The coinage of Maria Theresa, 'Queen of Hungary and Bohemia, Countess of Tyrol, Archduchess of Austria, Duchess of Burgundy and Empress of the Holy Roman Empire' circulated throughout the Austrian domains for almost forty years. Her magnificent silver thalers however, travelled far beyond her realms to places unknown to the Empress herself and were to immortalize her after her death in 1780.

Representations on the coins of the young queen reflected the spirit of a new era, and in due course all the great events of her reign were illustrated through coinage and commemorative medals. One of her first thalers, dating from the beginning of her reign in 1741, depicted her

---

Left:

An early thaler from Maria Theresa's reign dated 1742. The obverse shows the young queen as the embodiment of youthful charm.

Above:
The reverse of the 1742 Maria Theresa thaler depicts the Madonna and child. It reflects the religious authority of the Empire and was an image which circulated widely throughout the Islamic world for many years.

with the classical features of the Roman goddess Minerva, the traditional protectress of people and lands. This rather impersonal effigy, which came from the mint in Vienna, soon gave way to a more lifelike portrait, and throughout the 1740s the youth and vulnerability of Maria Theresa was reflected in her delicately-carved features. By the 1750s the royal image looked more assured, and her famous double chin made its first appearance, adding a touch of maturity to her image. The pronounced Habsburg underlip which, it was hinted, she had inherited and which was so prominently portrayed in the portraits of her male ancestors, is nowhere in evidence, and contemporary portraits of the Empress gave no sign of it.

Maria Theresa's hair was her crowning glory,

and it was said she was proud – and rightly so – of her abundant golden curls. The engravers and artists who worked on her early coins certainly did it justice. She was shown with cascades of finely carved ringlets intertwined with diamonds and pearls. Many years of engraving sumptuous imperial wigs had given generations of medallists great proficiency in this area. The same expertise was extended to depicting the bodices of her lavishly-embroidered gowns with their swathes of lace and ermine. The reverse of the coins showed the impressive Habsburg arms with its intricate display of escutcheons surrounded by crowns, swirling feathers, and a ferocious double-headed eagle.

Maria Theresa's husband Francis Stephen, elected Holy Roman Emperor in 1745, was crowned with enormous pomp and ceremony in Frankfurt. Maria Theresa was then able to use the title of Empress. An abbreviated form had to be fitted in along with all the other titles which encircle her coin. Lappets of armour at her shoulder signified her new status and merged incongruously with the silken folds of her embroidered gown. The florid effigy of the Emperor showed him wearing armour and a laurel wreath half buried among the abundant curls of his wig.

A number of Imperial State mints were operating throughout the extensive Austrian lands in the eighteenth and nineteenth century. Housed in large handsome buildings constructed especially for the purpose, they were usually situated near a river or canal in the centre of a city. From 1751 Maria Theresa's coinage was struck in the mints of Vienna, Karlsburg in Transylvania, Kremnitz in Hungary, Hall in the Tyrol, and Prague in Bohemia. In 1764 a mint was opened in Gunzburg, a small town in

Right:

This thaler of 1765 depicts the Empress with a more mature figure, showing the beginnings of a double chin, and wearing lappets of armour at her shoulder, which signify her Imperial status. As a female she could not inherit the title Holy Roman Emperor and it was only after her husband was elected Emperor in 1745 that the title Empress appeared on her coins.

Below:

Thaler of the Emperor Francis struck in the 1740s. His coin circulated abroad for a time concurrently with that of the Maria Theresa thaler but was not as long lived, nor as popular. In Ethiopia it was offered at a discount. If the surface of the coin was at all worn and the Emperor's image indistinct it could be mistaken for the coin of his wife.

unlikely ever to have seen in person. As each die was engraved by hand it was inevitable that minor variations occurred in the various issues of the thaler.

A coin is made by striking a flat piece of metal, called a blank, between two dies which have a design cut into them in reverse. In the case of an eighteenth century silver coin, the

Bavaria, and from 1820 to 1866 mints in Venice and Milan also produced Maria Theresa thalers. Each mint had its own engravers who worked from a portrait of their subject, whom they were

Hotel impl. des Monnoies rue. N° 92. Das k.k. Münz-Gebœude in oer, oit Himmelpfortgafse. Himmelpfortgafse.

metal was first melted then cooled into ingots, after which it was put through a rolling mill to be pressed into the desired thickness. The dies themselves were made from iron or steel and in the early days of struck coinage, the design had to be carved into this unrelenting metal by hand, a hugely demanding task considering the small size of the coin. The fine details had to be carved in negative in order to create a die. Great skill was required, and a very steady hand. As the dies had only a limited life, the whole process of cutting new ones had to be repeated when the old ones became worn.

The craft of coin or medal engraving was

Above:

An eighteenth century engraving of the Imperial Mint in Vienna. Once the Winter Palace of Prince Eugene of Savoy, it was purchased by Maria Theresa in 1753. The Mint was housed there until 1837, after which it was relocated to its present site.

exacting and highly skilled work which combined an artistic sensibility with technical expertise. It not only took its toll on the eyesight but brought on arthritis of the wrist. Only after many years of arduous apprenticeship as a *graveurscholar* could a young man expect to be promoted to the position of an assistant engraver. Within the Habsburg Empire it was a peripatetic existence: if the apprentice proved especially proficient, after years of painstaking toil, there might be promotion to the position of chief engraver at one of the many Imperial mints. Becoming Mint Master was the summit of achievement for an engraver, and only the exceptionally talented reached those heights. Dynasties of medallists, coin engravers and mint officials were not uncommon and, in the time of

Maria Theresa's reign several generations of the Wurchsbauer family were closely involved in the production of her coins and medals. According to Leonard Forrer in his *Biographical Dictionary of Medallists* (1905), Franz Ignaz Wurchsbauer, a graduate of the Graveuracademie was appointed assistant engraver at the Vienna Mint in 1744. From there he was transferred to Kremnitz, then to Hall, and finally to Graz. He was succeeded by his cousin Johann Baptist Wurchsbauer, who became Mint engraver at the Gunzburg Mint, where he engraved the dies for the Levantine thaler. His annual salary was eight hundred florins. Another member of this family, Karl Wurchsbauer, was working at the Karlsburg Mint on the dies for Maria Theresa thaler restrikes in 1805. Unfortunately his work proved less than satisfactory: the chief engraver, a man named Harnisch, complained of his carelessness and declared that, compared with the products

Below:
In the eighteenth century the actual striking of the coin was done using a screwpress operated by four or more men. The most hazardous job was that of the operator who held the blank in place and ran the risk of losing a finger or two in the process.

M. Ledeli. Der Prägesaal in der Wiener Münze.

Above:
The minting hall of the Vienna Mint in the nineteenth century.

Opposite:
Eighteenth century coining tools for the Maria Theresa thaler.

of all other mints, the Karlsburg thalers were the least well made. Matters did not improve, and Karl was later officially censured for unseemly conduct towards the mint officials and summarily pensioned off.

The invention of the reducing machine in France towards the end of the eighteenth century brought a huge advance in the production of master tools, and made the whole process of coining quicker and more efficient. It enabled the engraver to carve the design in relief in plaster or some soft material, on a much larger scale. The machine, by tracing the outline of the design, simultaneously cut a reduced version in hard metal. The result was a master 'punch' which could be used to make repeat dies when needed. This welcome invention was not available during the reign of Maria Theresa, and all her coinage was produced using hand-engraved dies. It was a testament to the skills of engravers that they were able to produce such impeccable examples.

A visit to the extensive coin rooms housed in the Kunsthistorische Museum of Vienna gives an insight into the rich history of the Habsburg Empire. In addition to the coinage of Maria Theresa, there is a dazzling collection of medals which were issued during her reign. These celebrate her wedding in 1738, her coronations in Pressburg and Prague, military victories and the many births and deaths within her extended family. There was even a medal to celebrate the Empress's recovery from smallpox in 1767.

With the sudden death of the Emperor Francis in 1765, his distraught widow went into a period of deep mourning. Her coinage then portrayed her heavily veiled, and in place of the voluptuous Empress, there was a grieving widow enveloped in a forbidding mantle. Her sole ornament, the tiara, was partially concealed by the veil covering her head. The Empress never recovered from her great loss: thereafter she took to wearing black and covered her beautiful hair for the rest of her life.

But her thalers tell a contradictory story. In 1772 she emerged, in silver at least, more resplendent than ever, her widow's weeds thrown aside and her legendary bosom restored to its full glory. A light veil now fell in soft drapes down the back of her head and an ermine stole was fixed at her shoulder with a brooch.

The reasons for this change in her iconographic representation have attracted much speculation over the years. It would appear that the money dealers and merchants of the Levant were dismayed by the effigy of the Empress in her widow's weeds and rejected unanimously that version of the coin. They begged the Gunzburg Mint to restore their old familiar version of the thaler which had been accepted everywhere so readily. It was vital that the image

Above right:
A Maria Theresa thaler of 1768, showing the Empress wearing widow's weeds after the death of her husband in 1765. Although she was not yet fifty, the Empress remained in semi-mourning for the rest of her life, eschewing the sumptuous gowns and jewels she had worn with such elegance, replacing them with simple dark clothes.

Below right:
A Maria Theresa thaler of 1773 minted in Prague. The image of the heavily-veiled Empress was not popular with the Levantine merchants and a new design was produced which depicted her wearing a lighter veil and a low cut gown.

on the coin should remain consistent at a time when it was just becoming established as a medium of exchange abroad. Other coins had lost their reputation when their appearance had been altered.

But were there other reasons for the change? It has been hinted that what the Levantine merchants really favoured was the image of the large bosomed Empress, with an emphasis on her low-cut gown. Was the latter image considered to be more successful commercially than that of the heavily veiled widow? It is tempting to think so. On the other hand, would the bedouin in the deserts of Arabia, or the trader deep in the interior of Africa have seen it in this way, for it is unlikely that many of them had even seen a European female by the late years of the eighteenth century. Their main concern was probably not the Empress's alluring bosom, but the much more critical issue of the number of pearls in the brooch, or the diamonds in her tiara, or the initials S.F., details which signified that the coin was genuine.

SCOT-
LAND

SWEDE

NORTH
SEA

DENMARK

HANOVER

BRANDENBU

Berlin

ENGLAND

Amsterdam

UNITED
PROVINCES
(HOLLAND)

London

SAXONY

Dresden

Antwerp

RHINE

Brussels

Frankfurt

Prague

BOHEMI

AUSTRIAN
NETHERLANDS

BAVARIA

Paris

LORRAINE

Gunzburg

Augsburg

Linz

BREISGAU

Munich

AUST

FRANCE

SWITZERLAND

Innsbruck

Hall

TYROL

CARINTH

STY

Gra

CARNIO

BAY OF
BISCAY

VENICE

Trie

Milan

SAVOY

MILAN
(LOMBARDY)

Venice

RHONE

Parma

MODENA

Genoa

N

GENOESE
REPUBLIC

Florence

Leghorn

TUSCANY

PAPAL
STATES

Marseille

MEDITERRANEAN SEA

CORSICA
(to Genoa)

Rome

The Habsburg Lands
in 1740
with subsequent Imperial Mints

BALTIC SEA

EAST PRUSSIA

RUSSIA

Riga

Warsaw

VISTULA

POLAND

Kiev

DNIEPER

LESIA

Cracow

Kremnitz

Vienna

Pressburg

Budapest

HUNGARY

Karlsburg

DANUBE

Odessa

BLACK
SEA

Bucharest

Belgrade

OTTOMAN
EMPIRE

Ragusa

Constantinople

DRIATIC SEA

TWO
CILIES

Imperial Habsburg mints

V

THE LEVANTINER

*I*t is a sound business to export silver; for wherever they [the merchants] sell it they are sure to make a profit thereof.

Xenophon
Ways and Means

A brilliant piece of marketing strategy set the Maria Theresa thaler off on its career as an international coin. The person credited with launching the thaler abroad was the gifted Swiss financier Count Johann von Fries (1719-1785). His entrepreneurial qualities gained him entry into Austrian court circles where he won favour with Maria Theresa who entrusted him with various commercial ventures throughout her vast Empire.

Although from the outset there had been an official ban on the export of Maria Theresa thalers, in 1752 the Austrian Department of Commerce decided to lift the restriction as they considered it would help the country's negative

balance of trade with the Levant, and substantial profits could be made from the high agio (profit made when converting currencies) of the coin when traded abroad. Records show that from 1751 to 1761 some 17 million thalers were struck at the mints of Vienna and at Hall in the Tyrol; at least three million were made with von Fries's silver. Within twelve years he had sent eight million thalers into the Ottoman Empire from which his bank made a very substantial profit. These distinctive coins came to be known as Levantinethalers or Levantiners.

The silver was supplied by von Fries and other international bankers who came from Augsburg, a town close to Gunzburg. Four distinct types of thaler were minted at the Gunzburg Mint and have since come to be distinguished in the following terms by coin specialists: the armoured bust, the convention bust, the heavily veiled bust, and the lightly veiled bust. Examples of all of these may still be found in the *souqs* of Arabia and in parts of Africa where once they circulated.

Left:
Count von Fries successfully secured a monopoly on the shipment of all Maria Theresa thalers to the Levant and thus established profitable connections with merchants in that region.

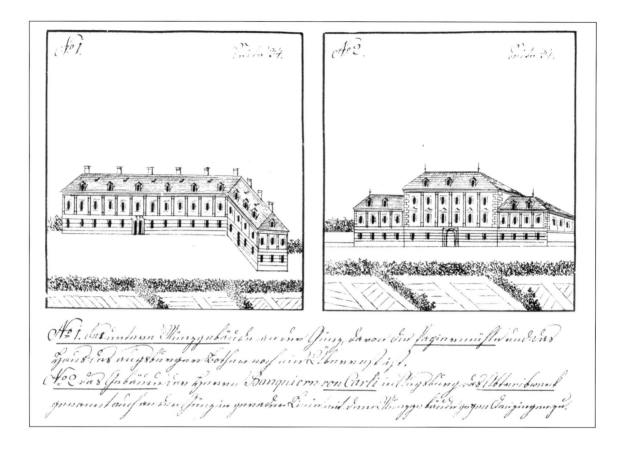

It is customary that on the death of a ruler his or her coinage ceases to be struck and the coin dies are normally destroyed. This is what happened to the many other Theresian denominations in circulation such as kreuzers, ducats and liards. The Levantiner, together with the half-thaler, was an exception to this rule because of its popularity abroad as a trade coin. The situation was further complicated by the fact that Maria Theresa's son Joseph had been acting as co-regent since the death of his father, and his own coinage circulated alongside that of his mother for nearly twenty years.

In the year after her death an order for Maria Theresa thalers arrived at the Gunzburg mint via the Augsburg bankers, who had trading links with the Levant. Permission had to be sought from the Emperor Joseph II for the order to be sanctioned. He had the foresight to realise that

this was potentially a very profitable business, and he gave permission for the coin to continue to be struck, with the proviso that the silver should be supplied by the customer. The dies used in the production were the ones already in use at the time of the Empress's death, with the date of 1780.

The Gunzburg mint enjoyed brisk business during the last decades of the eighteenth century as it met the demand from abroad. The coins were used by various European countries for their trade with the Levant. The French, for example, were forbidden to export their own currency at this time and resorted to Maria Theresa thalers to pay for their silk imports. Much of the demand, however, came from the coffee merchants of the Levant who needed to pay for their imports from Arabia. In 1805, Napoleon abolished the Holy Roman Empire and the mint at Gunzburg was closed. It had produced nearly 20 million Maria Theresa thalers since it first opened in 1764.

After 1780 several other Habsburg mints, notably Vienna, Hall, Karlsburg, Prague and Kremnitz, continued their output of Maria Theresa thalers up to the first quarter of the nineteenth century with the date frozen at 1780. The mints in Milan and Venice also produced thalers, before both cities were lost to the Habsburgs in the 1860s. Although the Maria Theresa thaler was demonetized in Austria and Hungary in 1858, an Imperial edict of 1857 allowed for the continuation of these restrikes for use in foreign trade. After 1867, Vienna became the sole mint in the Empire to strike Maria Theresa thalers. Here, with the exception of short periods during two world wars, production has continued until this day. The twentieth century saw the mints of Paris, London, Birmingham, Bombay, Brussels, Rome and others producing identical copies of the 1780 Maria Theresa thaler. Approximately 400 million have been struck since 1780. Some estimates put the number as high as six hundred million, if various unofficial mintings are taken into account. The Vienna Mint, the successor to the Vienna Hauptmünzamt is now a privately owned company housed in a handsome nineteenth century building in the heart of the city. Austrian Mint officials are justifiably proud of their world-renowned coin, which is looked upon as a type of mascot. They call it their *äufhangerschild*, a word that signifies an advertisement or sign hanging outside the premises of a business.

The Mint has no plans to stop producing their famous coin. In the course of most years, depending on demand, there are one or perhaps two mintings, and between 1998 and 2001 nearly 60,000 thalers were struck. There has been a steady demand over the years, mainly from coin dealers around the world. Advertisements appear in newspapers, magazines or on the internet. The Mint offers a choice of either the slightly more expensive proof coins, which have a cameo-like portrait in frosted relief against a mirror-bright background, or the more standard 'bright uncirculated' type. Prices vary from supplier to supplier, but in general one should not have to pay much in excess of the coin's current silver value.

The Maria Theresa thaler of 1780 has been the focus of attention of several eminent numismatists who have provided valuable insights into the complexities of the restrikes in several learned publications. The most comprehensive study is *Der Maria Theresian Taler 1780* (Wiener Neustadt, 1976) by

THE 1780 RESTRIKE

Maria Theresa thalers made after the Empress's death but stamped with the date of 1780 are properly classed as 'restrikes'. Sometimes they are known as the 'Maria Theresa thaler 1780' to distinguish them from the earlier versions. But the term Maria Theresa thalers or dollars is now in such common use for referring to the restrikes, and the disparity in numbers between the protoypes and the restrikes is so enormous that in this book the term Maria Theresa thaler refers to the pre-1780 coins as well as to the restrikes.

Below:

A rare Maria Theresa thaler from the Prague Mint struck in the year 1780. It has 11 diamonds in the brooch and on the reverse are the initials EvS-I.K. This example represents the prototype for the restrikes which were produced in the years following the death of the Empress.

Several engravers working in different Habsburg Mints were involved in the making of dies for the Maria Theresa thaler from 1780 onwards, and inevitably this led to variations in the detail on the coins, particularly in the first two decades. A number of well-documented and very obvious differences can be found between the various restrikes: there are some which bear only minor differences, and others that are almost undetectable. Any one of these discrepancies may provide clues as to the possible place of minting, or the approximate date of a restrike. These restrikes represent the most complicated aspect of the Maria Theresa story, and for a collector or a numismatist the challenge of searching for new variations is an exhilarating experience, making the thaler a fascinating and rewarding subject of study. To learn the distinguishing marks of the many restrikes and to work out their approximate date, or which mint they come from, requires persistence and great attention to detail.

THE 1780 RESTRIKE

While some of the variations illustrated below may have occurred by accident, quite often they were intentional: an issuing mint might deliberately have allowed one or two small differences to appear as a type of 'signature'.

There were times when these seemingly insignificant differences, such as a diamond less or more in the tiara, had repercussions abroad, as users of the coin were suspicious of any thaler that did not show all the standard features.

The Brooch

One of the most remarked upon features of the Maria Theresa thaler of 1780 was the oval brooch worn on the Empress's shoulder. Many of the early restrikes showed this brooch plain and unadorned, whereas others appeared with pearls surrounding it. The 1780 version which we see today has nine pearls, but due to a whim or a mistake by one of the engravers in the early nineteenth century, some of the issues appeared with 11 pearls. Others, mainly from Milan and Venice, appeared with a round rather than an oval brooch. These are some of the small

differences created by engravers and probably not noticed at the time, but which have assumed great importance, particularly amongst collectors. At the same time these variations provide a reliable way of dating some of the early issues. In the 1930s the mint in Brussels struck several thousand Maria Theresa thalers without any of the customary pearls, a situation that caused havoc in Ethiopia, where people using the coin insisted that all the details on it should be unchanged. As a result, all these Brussels restrikes had to be withdrawn.

The Habsburg Arms

Left:
The arms of Upper Austria were used from 1780-1820.

Right:
The arms of Burgau used from 1781 until the present day.

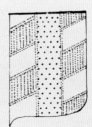

The Initials

Eventually all Maria Theresa 1780 restrikes were to carry the initials S.F., which represented the initials of the surnames of the mintmaster Tobias Schobel and warden of the Gunzberg mint Joseph Faby. In the years following 1780, when the thalers were being restruck at several different mints, the initials of other authorities appeared for a short period and are a reliable indicator of the issuing mint. Their rarity value makes them much sought-after by collectors.

These other initials include:

I.C.-F.A.	Vienna Mint	EvS-I.K. and P.S –I.K	Prague Mint
A.H-G.S	Karlsburg Mint	T.S.-I.F.	Gunzburg Mint
S.K.-P.D and A.S	Kremnitz Mint	VC-S	Hall Mint

The Saltire

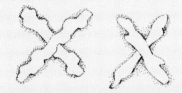

This is the St Andrew's cross which appears on the reverse of the coin after the date 1780 and was considered a stamp of authenticity. In this distinctive feature, the form of two crossed staves varies in shape and angle.

The Tiara

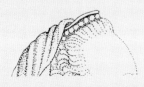

This item of royal regalia, which held the Empress's veil in place, depicted the precious stones either rounded or diamond shaped. The number of stones varies between five and eight.

The Edge Inscription

The Latin motto 'JUSTITIA ET CLEMENTIA' is interspersed with rosettes and arabesques which vary in style and length.

Tail Feathers

The tail feathers of the eagle varied in number. Dies from the London Mint, for example, had only two central feathers instead of the usual three.

Above:
Walter Hafner of Vienna, collector and world expert on the Maria Theresa thaler.

F. Leypold. This thorough account is an important resource for research on the subject of the restrikes. J.S. Davenport, a specialist on European and African silver dollars, provides an invaluable typology and reference work for the Maria Theresa thaler in his *European Crowns 1700-1800* (Galesburg, 1961). An important study of this complicated subject was undertaken by M. Broome in a paper in the *Numismatic Chronicle* (London 1972). More recently, François Regoudy of the Paris Mint has produced a well-illustrated book, *Le Thaler de Marie Thérèse 1780* (Musée de la Monnaie, 1992). One of today's foremost experts on the restrikes is Walter Hafner of Vienna, a collector and scholar whose knowledge and enthusiasm is an inspiration to all collectors of the Maria

Theresa thaler. His privately-printed *Lexicon of the Maria Theresien Taler 1780* is comprehensively illustrated with photographs of all the restrikes known to date.

The arrival of the internet and advanced global communications means that a wealth of information about the Maria Theresa thaler is now available to all. Auction houses and coin fairs around the world remain the traditional meeting places for serious collectors, and the Maria Theresa thaler makes regular appearances at the sales. As a numismatic curiosity it continues to inspire great passion and intensity amongst those who collect and study it. By its very nature, and because it was restruck in so many places over such a long period, it will continue to attract coin enthusiasts.

In 1926, the Vienna Mint produced three solid gold Maria Theresa thalers, each weighing 51.87 grams. The British Museum is the fortunate recipient of one of these prized coins. It was presented by Mr S. Azavay, a British subject living in Vienna, and the representative of a bank which had the monopoly of the export of Maria Theresa thalers to Ethiopia. Another gold coin was presented to the ruler of Ethiopia, Ras Taffari Makonnen. The British Mint in Bombay is known to have produced gold Maria Theresa thalers, one of which was presented to

King Farouq of Egypt by King Abd al-Aziz Al Saud, and is now in a private collection. It is understood that in the twentieth century a mint in Switzerland struck a number of gold thalers which were sold in the United States. Examples have also come to light of gold coins possibly made using a rudimentary sort of minting machinery in the Yemen. These foreign strikings are not considered genuine by the Vienna Mint but this does not diminish their value and gold thalers fetch high prices in the sale rooms owing to their rarity. Gold plated versions from private sources also exist.

Below:
A solid gold Maria Theresa thaler.

GLOBAL MINT RECORDS

Table 1: Reported Mintages of Maria Theresa Thalers for Habsburg or Austrian Mints		
Years	**Mint**	**Mintage**
1741-1750	Habsburg Mints	Unknown
1751-1866	Habsburg Mints	82,719,621
1751-1781	Hall, Günzberg, Kremnitz & Vienna	30,681,337
1782-1866	Karlsburg, Kremnitz, Prague & Vienna	37,209,331
1820-1866	Venice & Milan	14,828,953
1867-1915	Vienna	115,495,163
1920-1929	Vienna	53,676,003
1930-1937	Vienna	3,794,165
1751-1937	All Hapsburg or Austrian	255,684,952
1946-1955	Vienna	109,739
1956-1970	Vienna	10,189,577
1971-1980	Vienna	25,497,186
1981-1990	Vienna	12,841,973
1991-1998	Vienna	493,028
1946-2000	Vienna	49,141,224
1751-2000	All Habsburg or Austrian	304,826,176

Sources: Pre-1945 – [Hans 1950]; Post-WWII – Austrian Mint.

These tables appear with the kind permission of Adrien Tschoegl and represent his amendments to the figures which appeared originally in his article 'Maria Theresa: a case of International Money' in the *Eastern Economic Journal* published in the USA in 2001.

There are no mint figures available for the first nine years of Maria Theresa's reign. This absence of statistics has led to a frequent misconception that Maria Theresa tallers were first minted in 1751. An illustration of the young Empress's effigy on a coin dated 1742 is illustrated in the chapter 'Imperial Thaler'.

The figures given above come from the official records of 15 different mints and while they appear to give the full picture there is still debate as to whether some other non-Austrian mints were involved in the production of the Maria Theresa thaler at one time or another. The mint in Florence may have been producing them in the early nineteenth century according to an article by Antonio Alessandrini in *World Coins* (1969) although there is little evidence for this. Another mint which has been cited as producing

Table 2: Reported Mintages of Maria Theresa Thalers for non-Austrian Mints

Years	Mint	Mintage	Sources
1890s	Birmingham	Unknown	Ofonagoro [1979] [1]
1935-1939	Rome	19,446,729	Italian Royal Mint records [2]
1937-1938	Paris	4,512,750	Hans [1950]
1936-1941	London	14,724,016	Regoudy [1992]
1937-1938	Brussels	9,845,000	Royal Belgian Mint
1939	Utrecht	116,050	Boegheim [1991]
1940-1942	Bombay	18,864,576	Stride [1956]
1946	Paris	5,522,750	Hans [1950]
1957	Paris	2,074,456	Behrens [1969]
1949-1961	London	5,435,054	Broome [1972]
1949-1955	Birmingham	3,488,500	Behrens [1969]
1954-1957	Brussels	1,150,024	Royal Belgian Mint
1935-1961	All non-Austrian	85,179,905	

Notes:

[1] The records of the output of the Birmingham Mint in the Victorian period provide no support for this claim (Sweeny 1981). Other research on mint production for West Africa also provides no support for the claim (Vice 1983). Of course, the absence of evidence is not evidence of absence.

[2] Giulio Bernardi (Italian Numismatic Association). Sources: Adrien Tschoegl, 2004.

Maria Theresa thalers is that of Marseilles. It is alleged that they were given permission to strike thalers which were destined for the Levant. However, in 1802 Napoleon refused to authorize their minting. The French numismatist Francois Regoudy also discounts the notion of a Marseilles minting. Leningrad is rumoured to have produced these thalers as well as the mint in Antwerp but there is no firm evidence to date to support these claims. One may never know exactly how many mints throughout the world produced or attempted to produce this most famous of Austrian coins. Demand for it in distant places led to it being imitated in varying degrees of exactitude.

The records above testify to the remarkable and quite unprecedented longevity of the coin. For over two hundred years it has been produced almost continuously, a true survivor amongst coins. The Austrian Mint continues to produce it every year and it remains a favourite collectors item. Its longevity is as remarkable as the sheer total output to date: an astonishing four hundred million, and quite possibly more.

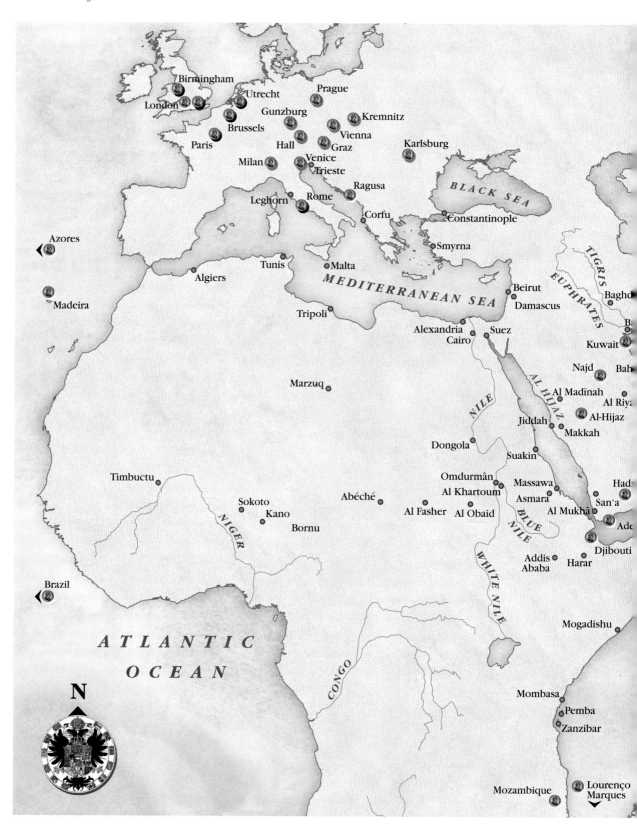

Birmingham
London
Utrecht
Prague
Gunzburg
Kremnitz
Brussels
Vienna
Paris
Hall
Graz
Karlsburg
Milan
Venice
Trieste
Ragusa
Leghorn
Rome
Corfu
Constantinople

BLACK SEA

Azores
Smyrna

Algiers
Tunis
Malta
Beirut
Damascus

MEDITERRANEAN SEA
Madeira

Tripoli
Alexandria
Cairo
Suez

TIGRIS
EUPHRATES
Baghd

Kuwait
Ba

Najd
Bah

Al Madïnah
Al Riy

AL HIJAZ

Al-Hijaz
Marzuq

NILE
Jiddah
Makkah

Dongola
Suakin

Timbuctu
Omdurmân
Massawa
Had

Al Khartoum
Asmara
San'a

Sokoto
Abéché
Al Mukhâ
Ade

Kano
Al Fasher
Al Obaid
Djibouti

Bornu
BLUE
NILE

NIGER
Addis
Ababa
Harar

Brazil
WHITE NILE

Mogadishu

ATLANTIC
OCEAN

CONGO

N
Mombasa
Pemba
Zanzibar

Mozambique
Lourenço
Marques

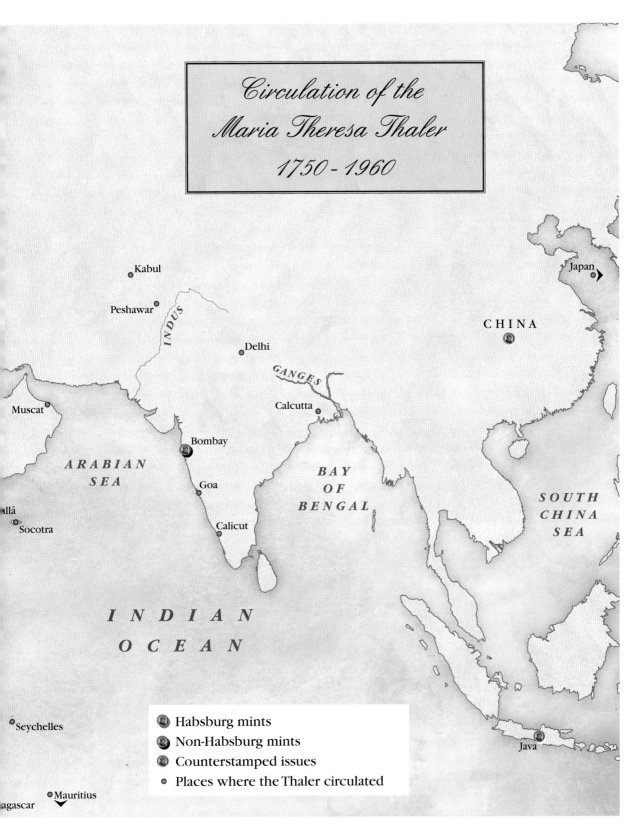

Circulation of the
Maria Theresa Thaler
1750 - 1960

Kabul
Peshawar
INDUS
Delhi
GANGES
Calcutta
Muscat
Bombay
ARABIAN
SEA
Goa
BAY
OF
BENGAL
Calicut
ḷḷā
Socotra
CHINA
Japan
SOUTH
CHINA
SEA
INDIAN
OCEAN
Seychelles
Java
Habsburg mints
Non-Habsburg mints
Counterstamped issues
Places where the Thaler circulated
Madagascar
Mauritius

銀銭 径リ一寸三分重サ十一銭五分表左向キ人頭花輪ノ銭巻
アリ下数字二字縁國字裏前ニ出ス十五銭八分ノ銭ト同
ジ疑ラクハ前ノ銭ノ小銭ナランカ

銀銭 大小二品大ナル者ハ径リ寸三分重サ七銭六分表
左向キ婦人ノ頭縁國字裏重鷲左右モニ背ヲ開ク首ノ外
偃月ノ形チ両翼両足左右ニ開ク尾乱ニ垂ル鷲ノ上小冠
アリ中央紋印十五立獅子三ツ獅子鷲蛇三鳥三冠石疊楯
筋斜筋等ナリ紋印ノ上ニ又冠アリ縁國字此類数品少キ

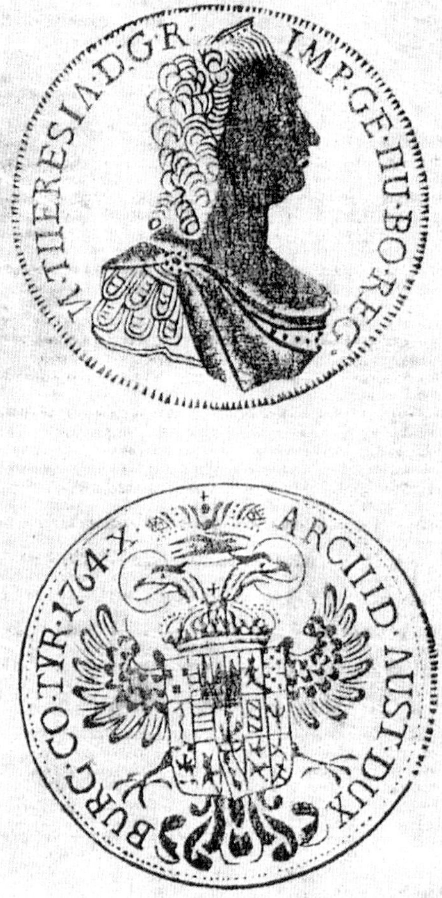

VI

A TWO HUNDRED YEAR REIGN

As they [silver and gold coins] are universal instruments of commerce, they are more readily received in return for all commodities than any other goods; and on account of their small bulk and great value, it costs less to transport them backward and forward from one place to another than almost any other sort of merchandise, and they lose less of their value by being so transported.

Adam Smith
The Wealth of Nations (1776)

It was Europe's passion for coffee that propelled the first of Maria Theresa's silver thalers towards their extraordinary destiny in Arabia and Africa. Coffee began to be cultivated in the highlands of Yemen in the 1500s, and from it a dark stimulating brew was made by roasting the green beans and crushing them. Sold in tiny cups by

Left:
A page from a rare Japanese coin catalogue of 1787 which gives a detailed description of the Maria Theresa thaler. The drawing shows a coin of 1764, an indication of its extensive global circulation.

street vendors and coffee houses throughout Arabia and the Levant, it was said to 'quicken the spirits and make the heart lightsome.'

The Austrians discovered the pleasures of drinking coffee after the Turks inadvertently left a sack of beans behind when fleeing after their unsuccessful siege of Vienna in 1683. By the eighteenth century, coffee houses were well established all over Europe. Lively meeting places, they were disapproved of by the authorities who feared that they might encourage conspiracies and seditious activities. In Muslim countries, religious leaders called for coffee houses to be closed down, as they kept people from attending prayers in the mosque.

Meanwhile, there was pressure to keep expanding the trade in coffee as the middlemen were making large profits.

The merchants of Yemen and Ethiopia exacted payment in silver for their prized coffee beans, which in turn led to the demand for a reliable silver coinage. Levantine traders, who controlled much of this trade from the sixteenth century, used a variety of European coins, the most popular being the lion dollar and the small gold Venetian sequin. They both vied with the Spanish dollar for a share in the immensely lucrative coffee trade. Coins of the Ottoman Empire, which was then in control of much of Arabia, had proved to be unreliable, of questionable alloy, and in short supply. By the late 1700s these coins began to be supplanted by Maria Theresa thalers, which gradually took over as the monetary standard in the Levant.

The Danish explorer Carsten Niebuhr was one of the first Europeans to encounter the Austrian

Above:
An 18th century engraving of coffee being cultivated on terraces in the Yemeni highlands. Coffee was a cash crop and was paid for in Maria Theresa thalers.

Opposite:
Carsten Niebuhr, wearing the local dress presented to him by the Imam of San'a. He is one of the first visitors to Yemen to have mentioned the use of Austrian thalers as currency in Yemen in 1762.

thalers in Yemen, when he visited the country in 1762. His party consisted of a philologist, a doctor, a botanist and an artist, with Niebuhr acting as surveyor, astronomer, and treasurer. In the final stages of the journey he became the leader as one by one his colleagues fell ill and died, and he found himself the only survivor. The years following his return to Europe were spent

collating the diaries of his erstwhile colleagues which, together with his own observations, were first published in 1772 in Copenhagen under the title *Beschreibung von Arabien (Travels in Arabia)*. His book stands as a written monument to those intrepid scientists who, despite the vicissitudes of their journey, brought to light many fascinating aspects of this little-known corner of southern Arabia. Niebuhr referred to thalers as 'German crowns', the name they were usually given in the accounts of contemporary travellers. He writes that, 'when it was noticed by the Viennese that more and more of their coins were finding their way to the Levant and particularly to Egypt, they reduced the fineness of their coins. The Yemenis soon noticed this and today give 5 per cent more for the crowns minted before 1756.' It was true that the silver content of Maria Theresa thalers had been very slightly lowered from 835 grams following a Monetary Convention with Bavaria in 1753. According to this agreement all silver thalers thereafter were to be composed of 833.3 grams of silver.

'The Arabs have scarcely any article for exportation, except coffee, of which the Indians are not very fond', remarked Niebuhr. This meant that ships trading between India and Arabia arrived heavily laden from India, yet returned with only substantial quantities of silver coinage. In one instance it is recorded that merchants had freighted an English vessel from Jeddah with one million crowns on board. 'These sums are almost always in European coins, Venetian ducats, or German crowns', wrote Niebuhr. 'It may be supposed that other English and Indian vessels carry also considerable sums from Jidda and Mokha. The ships which sail from Basra to India are in the same manner freighted with money which has passed from Europe through Turkey. When to this we add the quantity of specie carried directly to India and China by the nations of Europe, it appears that Europe must have been long since exhausted of gold and silver, were it not for the treasures imported from America.' European silver was indeed becoming scarce, and by the end of the eighteenth century it was silver from the Spanish colonies in America which was used in the production of European coins.

The growing appetite in Europe for luxury goods from the East led to an expansion of global trade from the Americas across to China and Japan, and new trading empires grew rich and powerful by gratifying the demand for such goods. Majestic dhows from India, borne by monsoon winds, arrived at the ports of southern Arabia and the Red Sea heavily laden with exotic products from the East such as cardamom, cassia, camphor, vermilion, and benjamin and attar of rose perfumes. Jeddah acted as an entrepôt for this trade since the Ottoman authorities, as custodians of the holy mosques at Makkah and al-Madinah, maintained the port as the centre where all merchandise was unloaded and taxed. The Ethiopian port of Massawa traded in slaves, ivory, gold, coffee, leather hides and ostrich feathers. From Zanzibar came scented cloves and more slaves; from Muscat came dates, Persian silk, shawls and carpets, while frankincense and myrrh came from the Hadramaut.

Below:
The Red Sea port of Jeddah: 'The commerce between Arabia and Europe meets here and is interchanged', remarked Major Henry Rooke, a visitor to Arabia in 1782. Maria Theresa thalers were carried into the interior by camel caravan or on to other Red Sea ports while others were sent to India.

Cargoes were trans-shipped into smaller vessels before continuing up the Red Sea to Suez, and thence through Egypt to Europe and the Levant. In this way Jeddah benefited from the complex system of duties, taxes and port charges levied on this trade. According to W. Milburn in *The India Trader's Complete Guide* of 1825, no ships from Mocha, Muscat, or India could enter any port north of Jeddah. On their return journey these vessels would be filled with luxuries from Europe such as Venetian glassware, mirrors, gilded perfume bottles, faceted crystal flowerpots for orange blossom, glass beads of many hues, steelware, and silks from Leghorn and Florence. Austria supplied needles, knives, haberdashery and the silver thalers which fuelled much of this trade, especially in goods which could only be exchanged for cash, such as slaves, coffee and ivory.

It suited Austria to export their silver thalers. The Habsburg lands were seldom able to export more products than they imported. Silver coinage was in short supply in much of Europe, and Austrian thalers fast became indispensable to the Levantine trade.

Above:
*A variety of different European coins circulated in
the ports of the Red Sea during the eighteenth
and nineteenth century.*

Commercial agents and bullion brokers residing in the ports of Trieste, Venice, Leghorn and Marseilles sent thalers off on the first stage of an eventful journey which took them across the Mediterranean to Egypt, a conduit for their journey to the Red Sea. Government records in the late eighteenth century reveal that the Egyptians also preferred payment in Maria Theresa thalers for all their transactions. From Egypt, thalers were traded along the north coast of Africa and penetrated into the Sahara and West Africa. Others were shipped to Constantinople and transported overland to Basra by camel caravan, and then along the Persian Gulf to Oman.

In transit by sea or overland, silver thalers were usually packed in lead-lined wooden boxes. They were subjected to inspections as the money merchants and traders who controlled and guarded their passage unloaded, scrutinized, counted, weighed, sorted and redistributed their treasure along the way. According to Milburn, port charges were high, and the whole process of selling your cargo was elaborate and lengthy. He detailed the complicated system of duties levied and the gifts required to soften up the 'nayibs, bashaws, viziers, sheriffs' *en route.*

Travellers to Red Sea ports in the eighteenth and nineteenth centuries report on the Byzantine nature of the currency arrangements. In Jeddah financial transactions were particularly complex because of the annual influx of pilgrims to Makkah and al-Madinah who flooded the towns with a bewildering variety of foreign coins. Large silver denominations from Europe such as thalers, crowns, sequins, pataks, ducatoons and pistareens were common currency. Smaller coins such as zermabobs, gingelees, commassees and stamboules were brought in to defray daily expenses and for alms giving. It was a chaotic situation, with coins of differing metals, weights, and sizes being exchanged. Pilgrims were at the mercy of money changers and were inevitably the losers. Prices rose steeply during the annual Hajj, exchange rates fluctuated daily, while every pilgrim was obliged to pay a pilgrimage tax which could be anything from ten to a hundred thalers.

All these financial transactions were dominated by the *serafs* or *schroffs* – money dealers – most of them Hindus from Gujarat in India. Perched behind their wooden money boxes, they controlled the local exchange rates, calculating supply and demand, the price of silver and the scarcity of certain coins. Ali Bey, a pilgrim from Morocco, writes in his *Narrative of a Journey* (1803) that, 'Every sort of money circulated in Mecca. Money changers sit in the market behind a little counter with a small pair of scales and are occupied all day in transacting their affairs in an incorrect way; but it may be imagined not to their own disadvantage.' Sometimes the *serafs* found the counting of coins too arduous and preferred to weigh them, though their scales were often unreliable.

Pilgrims converged on the holy cities by caravan or on foot along routes followed for centuries. They came from Bukhara, Samarkand and Anatolia together with dervishes from Persia, Damascus and Baghdad. Others arrived on crowded dhows from as far afield as Sumatra and China. Some travelled across the Red Sea from the far reaches of Muslim Africa, from Niger, Sudan, and the Maghreb. Many would have been on the move for months, and sometimes years, crossing the African continent from its western extremes, pausing *en route* to earn funds for the next stage of their journey. In order to help defray the costs of their passage,

Below:
Banian merchants from Gujarat settled in many of the Red Sea ports where they controlled much of the trade. As money changers they were known as serafs *or* schroffs *and were skilled in the art of monetary exchange.*

they brought goods to sell or exchange. During the pilgrimage, Makkah became a mart for carpets from Turkey and Persia, rare cloths from India and precious stones from Sri Lanka. Transactions were made in thalers, which were later borne off to distant lands by returning pilgrims.

The hajj attracted a number of European travellers who, because of the strictures on non-Muslims taking part, had to go in disguise. Jean Louis Burckhardt, a Swiss by birth, was one of the earliest. A gifted Arabist and resourceful traveller, he set off up the Nile from Cairo in 1812 and journeyed through Nubia, where he was the first European to see the half-buried ruins of Abu Simbel. Then, disguised as a pilgrim, he joined a caravan of rapacious slave traders who were *en route* to Jeddah. An average of 20,000 slaves passed through Jeddah annually on their way to Egypt, Arabia, and beyond. It was a journey fraught with danger, and Burckhardt endured terrible privations throughout. He managed to keep a diary, though he risked his life by doing so. Here he recorded the depravities of the slave traders and the suffering of the slaves whose greatest fear, it seemed, was that they would be eaten on arrival at the coast. Burckhardt owned a slave whom he was forced through lack of funds to sell on arrival in Jeddah. He had bought the slave for 16 dollars in the Sudan and sold him for 40 dollars, a profit that helped pay for his trip, though he regretted having to part with his trusted attendant. Burckhardt, who kept meticulous details of local currencies, reported that the Spanish dollar was the pre-eminent coinage in Sudan, where merchants who had brought them from Egypt sold them on for handsome profits.

'The Spanish dollar is most prized in Al Hijaz; in Al Yaman the Maria Theresa', wrote Sir Richard Burton in *Personal Narrative of a Pilgrimage to Al Madinah and Mecca* (1853), an absorbing account of his journey to the holy places of Islam in 1850. 'The traveller wonders how "Maria Theresas" still supply both shores of the Red Sea. The marvel is easily explained: the Austrians receive silver at Milan, and stamp it for a certain percentage. This coin was doubtless preferred by the *Badawin* for its superiority to the currency of the day: they make from it ornaments for their women and decorations for their weapons.' Milan was part of the Habsburg empire until the unification of Italy, and it is reported that the Milanese mint and the Venice mint produced Maria Theresa thalers from the late eighteenth century to the first decade of the twentieth century.

Every year, great trading caravans descended from the highlands of Ethiopia to the port of Massawa on the Red Sea, bringing gold, civet, rhinoceros horn, ivory, honey, rice, wax and large numbers of slaves. Like coffee, slaves were paid for in silver coins rather than in goods.

Traffic in humans had long existed between Africa and Arabia. Massawa, the island port of Ethiopia, prospered as a result of the export of slaves, as did Tripoli on the north coast of Africa and Suakin on the Red Sea coast of Sudan. The revenues of both Zanzibar and Muscat were based on this human cargo. Slaves from the eastern flank of Africa were mostly shipped to Arabia, Egypt, Turkey and Europe, the females becoming concubines and dancers as well as servants. Eunuchs were much in demand in the harems of various royal potentates and fetched the highest prices.

The prices for slaves listed in historical accounts of the nineteenth century were usually

SIR RICHARD BURTON

Burton (above) in the clothes he wore when travelling on the pilgrimage in 1853 wrote:

'I bought fifty pounds worth of German dollars (Maria Theresas), and invested the rest in English and Turkish sovereigns. The gold I myself carried; part of the silver I sewed up in Shaykh Nir's leather waistbelt, and part was packed in the boxes for this reason — when Bedawin begin plundering a respectable man, if they find a certain amount of ready money in his baggage, they do not search his person. If they find none they proceed to a bodily inspection, and if his waist belt be empty they are rather disposed to rip open his stomach, in the belief that he must have some peculiarly ingenious way of secreting valuables.'

prices for slaves in the middle of the nineteenth century:

A robust man	12-14 thalers
An old man	4-5
A middle aged woman	10-15
A bearded young man	15-18
A girl	20-25
A eunuch in boyhood	50-80

given in Maria Theresa thalers. It is disheartening to learn that the highest rate paid for a slave did not compare with the cost of an Arabian horse, which could fetch up to two thousand dollars. An elephant might fetch two hundred dollars, while a eunuch, the highest rating for any slave, would only fetch a hundred dollars. Women slaves were worth the least, and even the most sought-after Galla beauty from Ethiopia would only raise between twenty-five and forty Maria Theresa thalers.

Gustave Nachtigal, a Prussian physician who travelled through the central regions of Africa between 1869 and 1874, gives the following

Nachtigal's account of his journey to visit the Shaikh of Bornu, carrying with him a gold framed portrait of Frederick the Great as a gift for his host, includes a comprehensive account of prices in the market places he passed through, and gives an insight into how useful the Maria Theresa thaler had become for local trade: 'In comparison with other countries, market trading in Bornu is greatly facilitated by complete freedom of trade and commerce and by the introduction of an official unit of value …. the Austrian Maria Theresa dollar, and of the cowrie as a subsidiary currency. This is recognized with thankfulness if one has experienced how

extraordinarily tedious and time consuming it is in other countries to get possession of specific objects, since they require different exchange media, and one often gets hold of them only through a series of exchanges.' Nachtigal went on to relate how this economic strategy was introduced by a returning hajji who had been much impressed when he saw how trade in Jeddah had been transformed by the use of an

---

Below:

The Shaikh of Bornu. Maria Theresa thalers greatly facilitated trade in the market place of Bornu, although as the women of Bornu converted so many of them into ornaments, there were at times great shortages of the coin.

acceptable currency.

The Maria Theresa thaler proved particularly useful when it came to collecting the taxes that nomadic tribes were frequently obliged to pay. Ruling shaikhs were delighted to receive their dues in solid silver instead of the usual cattle or sheep. Richard Pankhurst comments in his *Economic History of Ethiopia* that in Ethiopia, coinage was a convenient form of wealth for tribal rulers and local chieftains, who used it for the purchase of firearms. The coming of money to Ethiopia also resulted in a significant increase in taxation: 'As long as taxes had been collected in kind in such articles as grain, cattle, salt, honey, butter, the amount that a chief could effectively use – or store – was fairly restricted, but with the advent of money there was no such limitation'.

Henry Levick, Her Majesty's Vice-Consul at Suez in 1853, noted that a sum of 30-40,000 pounds sterling in Maria Theresa thalers left Egypt for Arabia, Ethiopia and other parts of Africa in that year. By 1850, Maria Theresa thalers had been circulating as trade coins for a hundred years, and their diffusion was wider than ever. Where at first there had been suspicion and sometimes outright rejection of the thaler in Africa and Arabia, there was now a firm trust carefully fostered by the Levantine merchants, who were assiduous in their efforts to keep the coin unchanged in every minute detail. This was the key to its continuing popularity, to remain exactly as it always had been since 1780. From the mid-1800s onwards, statistics at the Austrian mints of Vienna, Milan and Venice indicate that there was an increase in the output of Maria Theresa thalers from a mere 123,000 in 1850 to nearly four and a half million in 1858. It was officially demonetised in the Austro-

Above:

In 1837 the British offered to buy the port of Aden for eight thousand Maria Theresa thalers, but when negotiations between Captain Haines and the Sultan of Lahej broke down they simply took it by force. The Governor General in Calcutta eventually agreed that the Sultan should receive an annual payment of eight thousand thalers. In the twentieth century Aden became an important entrepôt for the Austrian coins which were shipped to other parts of Arabia and across the Red Sea to Sudan and Ethiopia.

Hungarian Empire in 1858, but following a decree of 1857, it continued to be struck for use abroad. Despite the political and social upheavals in Europe and the Middle East between 1850 and 1950, the Maria Theresa thaler continued to circulate and even survived the final demise of the Austro-Hungarian Empire in 1919.

The next hundred years would see a phenomenal number of thalers flowing out from the port of Trieste, like a river of silver spreading across the Mediterranean into the interior of Arabia and Africa. It criss-crossed countries, not just along well-worn caravan routes but also in a maze of trails and dusty tracks. The opening of the Suez Canal in 1869 and the new era of steam navigation further aided its diffusion. India continued to absorb large amounts of silver from Arabia, most of which was melted down to make jewellery. Ghalib bin Awadh Al-Qu'aiti, the last sultan of the Qu'aiti state in the Hadramaut region of Yemen, and a notable scholar of Arab history, tells of quantities of Maria Theresa thalers being exported to India from Mukalla as late as the 1950s and '60s, and writes of trade in the coin in his own former territories from the middle of the nineteenth century. 'Whenever members of my grandfather's family travelled abroad, they would send trusted servants from Mukalla to Aden by dhow with boxes of thalers to exchange into paper currency. But convenience aside, the thaler was always considered superior. When silver prices were high it became worthwhile to send the coins to India for their bullion content. When prices fell, then the coins could easily be hoarded by burying them, and there was always internal demand for jewellery and dowry payments.'

The Qu'aiti family counterstruck the thaler in the 1880s to provide additional legitimacy to the coin in their territories. Of his own people and their journeys to Suez, the Hejaz, Ethiopia, India and Java, Ghalib Al-Qu'aiti writes that: 'They would often go by way of Jeddah, where they could board pilgrim ships. Many served rulers in India and elsewhere as soldiers, and acquired landholdings and wealth. Entrepreneurial families from Hadramaut built up prosperous mercantile interests in Java, which became one of the easternmost circulation areas of the Maria Theresa thaler.' Al-Qu'aiti adds that, 'Whenever I ask elders about the coin's history, they invariably reply *qadim jiddan* – 'it is very old'. Why did it spread and become so widely accepted? The reasons are complex. It took hold when Ottoman authority in the region was in decay. Their currency was largely unavailable because of weak administration, and people considered it debased and inferior.' This decline in Ottoman authority coincided with the intrusion of European powers into the Middle East and a consequential rise in trade.

The large commercial caravans that plied the age-old routes in the nineteenth and early twentieth centuries, between the bustling sea ports and great trading centres of the interior of Africa and Arabia, were ponderous affairs, with a medley of travellers and their beasts and a variety of trade goods swaying along in disordered procession. The draconian shaikhs who supervised these caravans wielded great power and enjoyed hefty profits. To them fell the responsibility for delivering the merchandise intact, and they saw to it that guards were posted day and night to prevent looting. A witness to

Opposite:
A thaler with the Qu'aiti stamp.

Right:
Ghalib bin Awadh Al-Qu'aiti, last Sultan of the Qu'aiti state in Hadramaut remembers immense quantities of Maria Theresa thalers being exported to India from Aden and other southern Arabian ports as recently as the 1960s. At the same time there was a continuing demand for them as dowry payments and jewellery within the country.

Below:
Elegant dhows departed from ports all along the Yemeni coastline loaded with heavy cargoes of Maria Theresa thalers, and crossed the Arabian Sea to India.

one of these caravans in Ethiopia in the 1920s was Charles Rey, a British diplomat. In his *Unconquered Abyssinia* (1923) Rey observed that: 'traders and travellers are for all practical purposes reduced to the use of the dollar, and every pound of coffee or wax, every hide or skin purchased in the interior must be paid for literally in hard cash – paper money, bills, cheques, etc., are of no value. So, in order to buy, say, 100 tons of coffee in the west country for shipment to the Soudan it would first of all be necessary to buy the requisite dollars in Addis - say some 32,000 dollars – load them on to mules and send them for a month's journey across country. And as the weight of these dollars would be about 2,000 lbs without packing, it would require over 20 mules for the purpose! I have myself seen a caravan of 30 mules laden in this way setting off for precisely this object.'

The value of thalers was assessed in terms of the current rate of silver. From Togo to Turkey the Maria Theresa thaler was traded as a commodity like any other, and therefore fluctuated in value according to local supply and demand. In addition, world silver prices became increasingly unstable in the late nineteenth century as country after country moved to the gold standard. This caused economic havoc, as the price of silver oscillated wildly. Money merchants were quick to take advantage of fluctuating prices to make profits, but they also suffered losses when prices plummeted. It was not simply the world silver price which affected the status of the Maria Theresa thalers. Their value rose or fell according to supply and demand, or through local conditions that were influenced, for example, by seasonal changes in crops during the year. Trade was limited during the hot season, when the price went up because fewer thalers were then in circulation. Sometimes there was a great scarcity of the coin, as for example in the First World War when minting of the thalers in Vienna was halted. Any political upheaval caused a scarcity, which in turn led to a rapid increase in price, and traders were quick to sell when the price was high, shipping thalers back to England in huge quantities in order to take advantage of the higher price of silver in London.

Maria Theresa thalers were not always appreciated everywhere, and there were times when their circulation riled and infuriated governing powers. For years the Ottoman government tried all sorts of strategies to oust

COUNTRIES & COLLECTORS

The Maria Theresa thaler was known as official or semi-official tender at different times in the following countries, (using the names by which they were known up to the middle of the twentieth century):

Albania, Algeria, America, Bahrain, Borneo, Cameroon, Central African Republic, Chad, Djibouti, Egypt, Eritrea, Ethiopia, Ghana, Greece, the Ionian Islands, Java, Kuwait, Lebanon, Libya, Malta, Mauritius, Moldavia, Morocco, Niger, Nigeria, Oman, Palestine, Romania, Saudi Arabia, Serbia, Somalia, Sudan, Syria, Tanganyika, Togo, Tunisia, Turkey, Uganda, United Arab Emirates, Yemen, Sultanate of Mukalla, Zanzibar.

As an international coin, it was little affected by changing borders and passed freely across continents.

Each country utilized it in its own way, depending on the prevailing economic situation, trading opportunities, or the whim of a ruler. In some places it became more entrenched than in others and survived for longer.

An interesting aspect of the wide-ranging circulation of the thaler was the manner in which various governments sometimes countermarked the coin with their own insignia, thus giving it the authority of state money. In some instances it acted like a hallmark, certifying that the amount of silver was correct and it was also a way of controlling coinage within a country.

As early as 1767 the Portuguese governor of Mozambique ordered all thalers in circulation there to be countermarked with the royal crown of Portugal, together with initials L.M for Lourenço Marques. This continued to be standard practice throughout the nineteenth century in the Portuguese dominions of the Azores, Madeira, Mozambique and Brazil, each country using a variation of the Portugese stamp.

The mark or stamp was generally applied to the obverse of the coin using a hand-held punch. As it is relatively easy to make forgeries of these punches, the result is that some of the stamps are of dubious authenticity. Countermarked coins can fetch high prices in the salerooms and care must be taken to ensure that the stamp is not a crude imitation.

Francisco Carbone, the Italian Consul-General in Aden in the 1960s, served in the Italian Legation in the Yemen from 1931, first in San'a, then in Tai'z. During his long period of service he assembled a collection of thalers which have proved of great interest to those studying the history of the coin, especially as this collection was put together quite randomly. The earliest Maria Theresa thalers from the Vienna Mint in the collection are dated 1754, and mintings from most years thereafter are represented up to 1780. The collection includes thalers of the Empress's husband, Francis Stephen of Lorraine, dated 1763 and thalers of Maria Theresa's grandson, Francis II, with dates from 1810 to 1830. There are no thalers of Maria Theresa's sons Joseph and Leopold, although that is not to say they were not in circulation. To this day a range of Habsburg thalers can still be found in many of the *souqs* of the Middle East, particularly in Yemen and Oman.

Left:
This coin has been marked to indicate that it is no longer legal tender.

them from the countries under its control, as in the Hejaz region of Arabia for example, where they were keen to promote their own similar sized coin, the mejidi. Thalers were banned by decree, and seized by the Turkish authorities, causing the price to soar. Those who refused to accept the mejidi ran the risk of being flogged. All these efforts were to little avail however, and the thaler remained a favourite with the local population, who clung on to it for as long as they could. Much the same happened in the Sudan when the Egyptian authorities, as the governing power, declared it illegal tender, an order that was generally ignored. The German tactic of preventing all importation of the coin into Tanganyika, Togo, and the Cameroons was more effective. These preventative strategies only proved how deeply entrenched the thaler had become in Africa and Arabia.

During the early twentieth century, the Maria Theresa thaler remained in demand on both sides of the Red Sea. In Ethiopia and Eritrea it was integral to the social, political and economic fabric of life. It had a particular place in the hearts and minds of the Ethiopian people, particularly those who were Christian. The image of the Empress together with her name, Maria, reminded people of the Virgin Mary. It was known as 'woman dollar' or *sett birr* in Amharic. Attempts to introduce the silver Ethiopian dollars of the Emperor Menelik (1889-1931) were not a success and people insisted on keeping the old Habsburg coin.

As new countries came into existence or gained their independence from colonial rule, governments created their own national currencies. They commonly imitated the Maria Theresa thaler as far as size and weight were concerned. Surface decoration was very different, especially in Islamic countries where human images were not used, and the design on coins was composed of verses from the Qur'an and geometric patterns. In 1924, Yemen started to mint its own silver riyal in the same size and weight as the thaler, but as there were never sufficient quantities of the riyal in circulation, the Imam Yahya bin Muhammad al-Din and his successor, the Imam Ahmad, bought Maria Theresa thalers from the money changers in Aden and over-stamped these as a national coinage.

In 1928 the ruler of the newly-created Kingdom of Saudi Arabia, King Abd al-Aziz Al Saud introduced the riyal; thereafter Maria Theresa thalers were no longer officially recognised as currency, although this did not prevent them circulating amongst bedouin tribes, and in the same year an order for half a million thalers was received at the Vienna Mint, apparently destined for the interior of Arabia.

In Oman the thaler traded freely together with the Indian rupee. When the new Omani riyal currency was introduced in the 1970s and the rupee officially withdrawn, the Maria Theresa thaler was allowed to remain in

circulation. It is still a familiar sight today in many of the marketplaces of Oman, mainly in silversmiths' shops where it is offered for sale as a souvenir or melted down for jewellery.

Slowly but inexorably, the two hundred-year reign of the much-loved trade coin drew to a close as demand for it began to dwindle. Yet statistics of the Austrian Mint show a sudden rise in demand in the last quarter of the twentieth century. Between 1976 and 1978, 22.5million thalers were minted in Vienna, and reportedly sent to Arabia. During this period the world price of silver soared as international rogue traders cornered the silver market. At the same time, and with chronic inflation gripping the Kingdom of Saudi Arabia, merchants and individuals in Jeddah and Riyadh frantically bought up Maria Theresa thalers. By January 1980 the price of silver had risen to the ridiculous value of 54 dollars an ounce. However, a few months later the great 'Silver Bubble' had burst and the hoards of thalers returned to their normal value.

Below left:
The tallero d'Italia dated 1919 which the Italian Government hoped would displace the ever-popular Maria Theresa thaler in Eritrea. The image on the obverse was clearly designed to resemble the Habsburg Empress although it proved unconvincing and like earlier attempts to introduce thaler-type coins, such as the King Menelik or King Umberto dollar, it ended in failure.

Below right:
In China silver coins were given chopmarks after their weight and fineness had been verified.

A COIN OF COSMOPOLITAN IMPORTANCE

And the old-established House of Habsburg have turned out for a century and a half, as though it were Rowland's Macassar Oil or a Bath Oliver biscuit, a thoroughly sound and reliable article, none genuine without the signature of the now long-sainted Mrs. M. Therese.

John Maynard Keynes (1914)

It is hardly surprising that Keynes, the foremost British economist of the twentieth century who led the British delegation to the Bretton Woods Conference of 1944, which set up the International Monetary Fund, should have commented on the phenomenon of the thaler. If the tone of Keynes's review of Fischel's *La Thaler de Marie-Thérèse: Etude de Sociologie et d'Histoire Economique*, is light-hearted, his assessment of the Habsburg coin and its economic vigour and longevity is assured. He argues that the Austrians anticipated one of Adam Smith's theses: that a country's money is no more than a commodity, and one able to take care of itself within the principle of supply and demand. He accepts Fischel's view of eighteenth century Austria as free from the mercantilist commercial ideas of the age, and the monetary protectionism of France, England and Prussia, who prohibited the traffic of coin, that is to say the practice of trading in coin for its intrinsic value rather than its exchange value, a trade that might lead either to hoarding, or melting down for other uses. And unlike its European counterparts, Austria had no imperial ambitions outside Europe. Though silver from Spanish-American sources was abundant in eighteenth century Europe, it was scarce in the Near East, a

condition that inhibited the use of silver money for exchange, or for hoarding, especially in remote districts. There was therefore a large and recurrent demand for foreign silver specie in the Near East, formerly met by the use of Spanish and Mexican dollars. The European powers competing to meet this supply were hampered either by their mercantilist policies, as in the case of France, or by the unreliable quality of their silver coinage, and the Austrians were able to step into this market with 'a handsome uniform coin of a high degree of fineness'. And while the thaler first entered the Near East through Levantine traders dealing in coffee and other products of Africa and Asia, the land trade in thalers through Egypt, Mesopotamia, Arabia, the Sahara and the Sudan was handled by Arabs, and Keynes argues that 'it was the taste of the Bedouin, therefore, that ultimately determined which of rival coins was to hold its own'. Keynes accepts Fischel's argument that it was the taste of the Arabs that explains the enduring popularity of the thaler in the Near East, where it became 'an object of aesthetic importance, of personal distinction and adornment'. In this context the durability of the thaler is further explained by the position of women in Arab society and 'their exclusive predilection for the image of the

Austrian Empress. In her coiffure, her jewelled pin, her massive bust and ample luxurious features, the Arab temperament finds its fullest satisfaction. And it is for these reasons primarily that the great lady has found her way to parts of Africa where no other white women has even yet been seen, and has remained married for many generations to the Arabian imagination. What we learn as the motto of her race in our school history books – *Bella gerant alii, tu felix Austria nube* (Others conduct business by means of war, you, fortunate Austria, by marriage) – has won another justification.'

Adrian E. Tschoegl, a more recent specialist in international money, affirms the importance of women in the Arab world in creating the demand for silver, 'where custom, or Islamic law, holds that a woman's jewellery, whether dowry, earned from her own labours, or a gift from her husband, remains entirely hers even in divorce.' This gave women an incentive to hold part of their wealth in the form of bullion variously transformed into jewellery. Tschoegl also sees the thaler as a unique phenomenon 'for its combination of longevity and geographical spread. It succeeded and survived not because it changed but rather because it did not'.

Tschoegl also sees the imperative behind the prohibition that the Imperial powers sought to impose on the thaler as a desire to extend the reach of imperial symbols such as national money, and to link them with local images in the colonies, a so-called civilizing mission that involved the introduction of a modern monetary system made up of standard units and their denominations to replace the use of commodity money such as the thaler. In addition a modern fiscal system would be more convenient than the use of silver-based money for large transactions, and answer the problem faced by many European explorers and travellers in Africa and Arabia and their complaints about having to carry large quantities of thalers on their journeys to facilitate their passage. However, the thaler proved remarkably resilient and its durability shows that in the history of the conflict between various bullion currencies there was a market preference for coins that were hard to forge and were of a high purity of silver.

Other economic historians have however argued that the thaler was 'a money of almost the highest perfection', explaining its wide circulation to the fact that it was not subject to the fluctuations in exchange rates of other currencies circulating in Austria and had a higher value in circulation outside than inside Austria. This was particularly evident after 1857 when the thaler ceased to be legal tender there but displaced silver coins abroad with a value lower than in their country of origin. This 'perfection' was however vitally dependent on Austria selling the coin abroad and never repurchasing it. As long as Austria remained the sole source of the thaler it continued to operate as money. As soon as the Italian and British governments began to strike the thaler themselves in 1935 and 1941 it ceased to operate according to the classic laws of sound money.

VII

A SILVER PASSPORT
TRAVELLERS' TALES

The Austrian dollar of Maria Theresa is the only large coin current in this country; the effigy of the Empress with a very low dress and a profusion of bust, is I believe, the charm that suits the Arab taste. So particular are these people that they reject the coin after careful examination, unless they can distinctly count seven dots that form the stars upon the coronet.

Sir Samuel Baker
The Nile Tributaries of Abyssinia (1868)

With these memorable lines, Sir Samuel Baker, one of the giants of African exploration, immortalized the Maria Theresa thaler. Sir Samuel and Lady Baker were passing through the Sudan at the outset of their momentous journey in search of the source of the Nile. Baker describes some of his encounters with the coin

with wry humour. In one instance he purchased the freedom of a local woman in order to engage her as a servant for the trip. He placed 35 Maria Theresa thalers in two piles upon the table, explaining that she was no longer a slave, as that sum had purchased her freedom, and that he expected her to remain with them until the journey was over, when she would receive a certain sum in wages. Under the impression that this was a marriage proposal, and overcome with gratitude, the woman embraced Baker effusively. She could only understand the concept of freedom in terms of becoming his wife.

Baker also writes of the minstrel who entertained him and Lady Baker one evening.

Left:
Festooned with delicately wrought silver ornaments, this Oromo woman sells her coffee beans in the open air market of Senbete in Ethiopia. In Arabia the coin is normally worn with the image of the Empress facing inwards.

73

Above:

Sir Samuel and Lady Baker were indomitable travellers who undertook long and hazardous journeys through the Sudan and Ethiopia. They learned the value of the thaler under many trying circumstances.

He was possibly a court musician, as he had been sent by a *Mek*, or local ruler of one of the small kingdoms along the Nile. The musician sang of Baker's deeds for at least an hour in a loud and – to Baker's ears – disagreeable voice accompanied by his fiddle. Baker thought that a couple of dollars would be ample recompense for this, and was startled to be told that 'a musician of his standing usually receives thirty to forty dollars from great people for so beautiful a song.'

Contrasting this with the price of a box at Her Majesty's Theatre in London, Baker lamented, 'I never parted with my dear Maria Theresa dollars with so much regret as upon that occasion.' The amount was disproportionate when compared to the price of a female slave, and one can only surmise that the musician must have been very highly regarded in his community, whatever Baker thought of his talents. In this incident it is likely that the noted explorer was paying dearly for the price of his fame, even in this remote region, and that all those who had been in on the act would have received their share of the profits from this performance.

Like many travellers to Arabia and Africa in the nineteenth and twentieth centuries, the Bakers were obliged to carry with them a certain quantity of ready money, usually in the form of

Maria Theresa thalers. They were needed not just for the purchase of provisions and porterage, but as gifts when buying favours from local warlords or for bribes in tricky situations. 'The all-powerful Maria Theresa thalers pay your way out of minor offences', wrote Rosita Forbes, who had many years' experience travelling in Africa. The Maria Theresa thaler was always more than a mere object of trade: it was often a useful instrument in smoothing a traveller's passage. Forbes argued that 'the real passport here is in silver and has a portrait of Maria Theresa', a point of view which nicely illustrates the role this illustrious coin played for the traveller in lands distant from Europe.

Most travellers acknowledged that thalers were a vital prerequisite for any journey into the interior of Arabia and Africa, and were grateful to have a commodity which could be readily exchanged everywhere. 'No one would look at anything but Maria Theresa thalers' declared Mabel Bent who, with her husband Theodore, visited Dhofar and Hadramaut at the end of the nineteenth century. She was the first European woman to visit southern Arabia, and her white skin caused surprise and revulsion amongst the tribes they encountered. Her account of their adventures, completed by Mabel after her husband's death, tells of constant demands for money from their bedouin guides. Acquiring thalers in the first place was not that simple, she discovered: 'You have to buy them dear, two rupees and a varying amount of annas, and are told they are very hard to get. They are tied up in bags, and you may very well trust the banker for the number of coins; but if you are wise you will examine them all, for any dirty ones or any that are the least worn or obliterated, or that have any cut or mark on them, will be rejected

and considered bad in the interior.' When it came to changing thalers back again on their return, they found that the coins had lost much of their value and were no longer in such demand, as Mabel ruefully noted.

Below:
Rosita Forbes made the first of her many adventurous journeys by crossing Ethiopia from the Red Sea to the Blue Nile in the 1920s. Although she found the Maria Theresa thaler an encumbrance it enabled her to buy her way out of many difficult situations.

'The most important preparation for the journey to the Yemen was the purchase of a large number of riyals or Maria Theresa dollars' asserted the entomologist Hugh Scott in his account of an expedition he undertook in 1937 in search of new species of insects. 'In Abyssinia years before, I had experienced how their value on the market would fluctuate from day to day, and the need of buying considerable amounts when they were cheap. In south west Arabia the fluctuations seemed less frequent, though of considerable extent. Soon after our arrival at Aden we bought a thousand riyals at the rate of about one and a half rupees per riyal, but in San'a, five to six months later they were obtainable at scarcely more than a rupee apiece. What memories are conjured up by these Maria Theresas, or Riyals Imadis (the official name in

Above:
Nigel Groom, a British political officer in southern Yemen in 1948, describes in Sheba Revealed, *how the Jewish silversmiths of Bayhan melted down Maria Theresa thalers and turned them into filigree jewellery for women and ornamental dagger sheaths for men.*

Opposite:
A thaler decorates the pommel of a saddle. Coins were frequently used as an embellishment on the hilts of swords and on matchlocks, rifles and shields.

the Yemen), or simply "birr" (silver) in Amharic, as my Abyssinians used to call them! Memories of going to the bank in Addis Ababa with two men bearing rifles and a porter carrying a big sack, to draw sometimes as much as a thousand dollars of the sacks full of thick shining discs, packed away in steel mule or camel-trunks (and the care to keep these always locked); or of a boot-bag pressed into service as a purse for some short trek of a few days.'

Celebrated explorers, such as Sir Richard Burton, went out to Africa and Arabia under the patronage of an august scientific organization such as the Royal Geographical Society and were usually furnished with a letter of credit or a written promise of payment, rather like a modern-day cheque, which could supposedly be exchanged for ready money in any large town or port. These letters of credit were often regarded with some suspicion, for even the most sophisticated local rulers were little acquainted with the concept of a promise on paper of payment sometime in the future. 'These people have no faith in notes – commercial, epistolary or diplomatic', remarked Burton. He was supplied with a letter of credit by the committee of the Royal Geographical Society and had requested that it should be as small as possible so as to fit into his talisman case. However, hindsight made him reconsider the size of the paper, and he later advised that such letters of credit should always be large and grand looking. In Cairo, Burton's Indian agents 'scrutinized the diminutive square of paper – the letter of credit – as a raven may sometimes be seen peering with head askance

into the interior of a suspected marrow bone. "Can this be a *bona fide* draft?" they mentally enquired. And finally they offered, politely, to write to England for me, to draw the money, and to forward it in a sealed bag directed to "Al Madinah." I need scarcely say that such a style of transmission would, in the case of precious metals, have left no possible chance of its safe arrival.'

Paying with the heavy silver coins was not always as straightforward as might be expected, and the process of counting them could be lengthy and tedious. Bertram Thomas, a political agent and explorer, gives an account of paying off his bedouin guides in Dakaka in southern Oman in the early 1930s. 'My camp table glittered with Maria Theresa thalers (1s 4d each), the only coin the sands know, and that but infrequently. The chink of silver, a sound rare in Dakaka, was a necessary accompaniment to setting up piles of 20s and 25s which would facilitate payment, for then all I had to do was to put so many piles into each man's hand as he came along. But I was reckoning without my host. Each laboriously counted and recounted his share and a horrid infection spread amongst them, each looking up and declaring he was one or two short. A companion would take the money out of his hand and count it back in fives, generally to the man's ultimate satisfaction. My method of counting – 6,7,8 etc, or even omitting to count at all puzzled them. Their practice was to count

Opposite:
The bedouin guides who led Bertram Thomas through the Empty Quarter were paid in Maria Theresa thalers, 'the only coin the sands know.' Each man was paid 50 thalers on the completion of the journey.

1,2,3,4,5 and then begin again – an object lesson in the appeal of the decimal system.'

The giving of change was a little known concept. 'If you buy a thing and they receive a greater piece of money, it is likely they will refuse to render the difference', wrote Charles Doughty in *Arabia Deserta*. It was universally understood that there was no change from Maria Theresa thalers unless one was prepared to accept bars of salt, glass beads, cowrie shells, or sundry other small items.

The lack of small change was a constant complaint except in Jeddah and Makkah, where the *souqs* were usually overflowing with small coins brought in by pilgrims. The introduction of a smaller coinage would have been very convenient but in the absence of small denominations there was nothing to do but pay with the valuable silver coin and expect to lose financially. Rosita Forbes was outraged by this state of affairs: 'The coinage of Abyssinia consists of Maria Theresa dollars, 80 per cent silver worth approximately three shillings each, of an incredible size and weight. A sack containing 50 pounds worth of these was as much as I could lift and four such bags form a mule load, but as there is no change in the interior, dollars are of little use except for a Croesus. You can buy 20 eggs or two chickens for a piastre and a sheep for three quarters of a dollar, but unfortunately all these coins are more or less mythical, and you have to go out into the market with your beautiful shining white dollars and haggle for piastres and quarters at an inflated rate.' In these circumstances it made sense to buy a sufficient number of items in order to receive one's money's worth. A German traveller recalled how he purchased coffee, sugar, salt, butter, soap, dates, some fresh vegetables, a sheep and twelve chickens from a Greek trader in Fashoda in central Sudan, all for the munificent sum of one Maria Theresa thaler. He could hardly have expected change from that.

Objects other than coins were often used as small change, and these would vary from country to country. European explorers to Africa took great quantities of glass beads with them, in addition to their supplies of thalers, and these were dispensed liberally as a way to ingratiate themselves with the local people whom they encountered on the daily march. Known as 'diamonds of Africa', they were much coveted by women as ornaments. Produced in Venice and Bohemia from the seventeenth century onwards, they were exported to Africa in prodigious quantities. They came in all sorts and combinations of colour, in intricate patterns and shapes. What was acceptable in one village might well be rejected in another, as fashions in beads changed from year to year.

Cowrie shells from the Indian Ocean had been a common form of currency from the earliest times, and provided a source of small change used in conjunction with the Maria Theresa thaler. These shells with their distinctive shape were sold by the string or, if the quantities were large, they were weighed out on scales. But currency was not their only function, for they were also coveted as fertility charms, and used to adorn all manner of objects from camel

Above:
A Baggara girl from the cattle-owning tribe of central Sudan. The leather trappings are adorned with cowrie shells which were used both as money and decoration throughout Africa.

Left:
Street merchants in Omdurman trade in glass beads from Europe. Beads provided the small change for the thaler; however trade in them could be dangerously speculative because their popularity was dependant on current fashions.

trappings to costumes. There is a tradition on the Musandam Peninsula in Oman for the sterns of the local fishing boats to be decorated with cowrie shells.

Salt was the preferred currency in Ethiopia before the arrival of coinage. Blocks of salt were more greatly prized than silver. An Ethiopian chieftain sold his horse for two hundred pieces of salt but, as this was not easily obtainable, ten Maria Theresa thalers were offered in lieu. The chief, far from pleased, replied that he would

keep the silver because it had been sent to him, but that in future he would prefer to be paid in salt, a rare instance of the Maria Theresa thaler not being appreciated.

The pitfalls of carrying large amounts of coinage on expeditions were obvious. Burton repeatedly warned of this, and advised against carrying boxes of thalers when travelling in a caravan, as bearers and local guides would become obsessed by the idea of treasure and would 'amuse themselves by lifting the case up and down and speculating on the probable amount of dollars contained therein.' On the evening halt, this precious cargo would be placed close to the owner so that he could keep vigil over it. Burton advised 'as a general rule always produce, when travelling, the minutest bit of coin', and not to display all your wealth. 'Above all things, the traveller must be careful never to change gold except in large towns, where such a display of wealth would not arouse suspicion or cupidity; and on no occasion when travelling even to pronounce the ill-omened word "kis"

Above:
Before silver coinage was introduced into Ethiopia, bars of salt were the most important form of currency throughout the country.

(purse). Many have lost their lives by neglecting these simple precautions.' Burton, who excels at describing the colourful and the unfamiliar, is never less than practical. 'I must not omit to mention the proper method of carrying money, which in these lands should never be entrusted to box or bag. A common cotton purse secured in a breast pocket, contained silver pieces of small change. My gold, of which I carried twenty five sovereigns, and papers, were committed to a substantial leathern belt of Maghrabi manufacture, made to be strapped round the waist under the dress. This is the Asiatic method of concealing valuables, and one more civilized than ours in the last century, when Roderic Random and his companion sewed their money between the lining and the waistband of their

Right:
For this Fulani woman from West Africa the safest way of keeping her wealth secure was to wear it around her neck while travelling.

breeches, except some loose silver for immediate expense on the road. The great inconvenience of the belt was its great weight, especially where dollars must be carried, as in Arabia, causing chafes and discomfort at night. Moreover, it can scarcely be called safe. In dangerous countries wary travellers will adopt surer precautions.' He does not say what could be safer than a money belt.

One way of counteracting this ever-present curiosity when on the move was to lay bare all that you owned at the very outset of the journey, a strategy that was recommended to Charles Doughty. The eccentric English explorer never felt at ease with the bedouin in Arabia, most of whom were Wahhabi Muslims and antagonistic towards Christians. The chronicles of his adventures, published in 1888 under the title *Arabia Deserta* and written in a somewhat archaic style, gives an unsentimental view of the country he passed through. Doughty kept his modest amount of coins in his medicine chest, but his guide, Saleem, insisted on counting every dollar in the box in front of several witnesses. He believed that everyone in the party should know exactly how much Doughty was carrying, as a safeguard against the event of his being accused of theft *en route* should any of the dollars go missing. As guide, he was responsible for the security of his client and would take all steps to anticipate trouble. 'Maabub told me, I should depart at evening with caravan men; and so he left me again. Then Saleem, with a mock zeal, would have an inventory taken of my goods –

and see the spoil! He called some of the unlettered cameleers to be witnesses. I drew out all that was in my bags, and cast it before them: but "*El f'lus, el f'lus*"! cries Saleem with ferocious insistence, thy money! thy money! that there may afterward be no question, – show it all to me Nasrany! – Well reach me that medicine box; and here, I said, are my few "reals" (dollars) wrapped in a cloth.'

Mabel Bent adopted the opposite tactic: she and her husband went to great lengths not to reveal all the money they had during their progress through different tribal lands in Arabia. 'We have become great hypocrites', Mabel declared. 'Our money being so bulky, was in bags scattered about among all the baggage, but we always had one store-bag in my box, and my husband had some for current expenses. The camel-men thought all the money was in a certain bag which was solemnly carried into the tent every night. While they shouted we filled the bag with a certain amount of dollars, meant to represent our entire fortune, and placed it on the table.'

Wilfred Thesiger enjoyed a much more trusting relationship with his desert companions. The twentieth century writer and explorer, whose epic journeys into the Rub' al-Khali, or Empty Quarter, of Arabia are recorded in *Arabian Sands*, writes that he found the lack of privacy during these prolonged desert crossings hard to endure although in time he grew accustomed to never being alone. 'It was very hard to hide anything from one's travelling companions when on a long trip. One was never really ever alone and there were eyes and ears everywhere, with the inevitable curiosity and speculation as to what treasure (if any) there lay stored.'

On his first crossing of the sands in 1946, he took with him in his saddle bag: 'a camera, a notebook, a volume of Gibbon and *War and Peace*, a press for plants, a small medicine chest, a set of clothes for bin Kabina ... and several bags of Maria Theresa dollars. These coins dated 1780, are still minted. They are about the size of a five shilling piece, are worth half a crown, and are the only coins acceptable here; the Arabs call

them riyals.' This money was kept in canvas bags tied with string, carried in unfastened saddlebags. 'My companions were desperately poor and yet the coins were as safe in my saddlebags as if they had been in my bank. I was five years with the Bedu and I never lost a single coin nor a round of ammunition, although this was more valuable to them than money.' Thesiger, who so effortlessly understood the sensitivities of his young companions gained their loyalty and trust on that first journey. He saw that they had made a leap of faith in trusting him, and he had to reciprocate. On his second crossing of the 'sands', which took him on a much more ambitious route, he helped his companions to load the camels. They took with them '200 pounds of flour, which was as much as we could carry, a forty pound package of dates, ten pounds of dried shark meat, and butter, sugar, tea, coffee, salt, dried onions and some spices. There were also two thousand Maria Theresa dollars, which weighed very heavily, three hundred rounds of spare ammunition, a small box of medicines, and about fifty gallons of water in fourteen small skins.' These were the bare necessities for such a long and difficult journey through the waterless Rub' al-Khali. He had a veritable fortune in thalers with him, substantially more than he had carried on the first journey, an indication of the seriousness of his undertaking.

The traveller Freya Stark considered it a measure of the improved security in Yemen when she could pass unguarded through the country carrying sacks of Maria Theresa thalers, although she preferred if possible not to carry cash at all. 'Of all the problems of travel in countries without a post office, that of money is the worst', she complained in *A Winter in*

Above:
A photograph taken by Wilfred Thesiger of his companions during his first crossing of the Empty Quarter in 1946-47. Thesiger remarked that his Maria Theresa coins were as safe in his saddle bags as if they had been in his bank. He took two thousand of them on his second crossing of the great sand sea of Arabia.

Arabia, which describes her travels in Arabia in the 1930s. Miss Stark wrote eloquently and with great perception about daily events in the lives of the villagers, especially the women and their families, most of whom lived in remote areas, where the only form of transport was mules. She feared being stranded without money; at least one delivery of Maria Theresa thalers was 'diverted' by a sheikh from a neighbouring village. Eventually Stark found the perfect solution. 'One cannot carry their weight on one's person, a strong box arouses more interest than is safe ... so the best way is to deal with the matter as the Arabs deal with it themselves, and to hand one's money bag and all responsibility to one's servant, who has a free mind to attend to it. I have now done this many times, nor ever had to regret it, for nine people out of ten respond to a trust that is placed in them, and the tenth ... one should have judgement to avoid.'

VIII

RIYAL NIMSAWI

T*he generic name for dollars is 'riyal Fransah'.*

Sir Richard Burton
Pilgrimage to Al Madinah and Mecca (1855-6)

During its two centuries of travel and adventure, the Maria Theresa thaler acquired a surprising number of names, titles, and epithets in various languages. If you were to ask for a Maria Theresa thaler today in a *souq* in the Middle East, your request would most likely be met with puzzled looks. If however you were to ask for a r*iyal fransah* in Yemen or Saudi Arabia you would promptly be rewarded with a clutch of Maria Theresa thalers from a dusty drawer.

When the thaler began to be used in trade beyond the borders of the Habsburg Empire in the 1750s its cumbersome Imperial title was changed to one that was more international. Appropriately, its first change of name was to the

---

Levantiner or Levantinethaler, a name which affirmed its status as a coin of commerce. This is how it was known by the merchants of the Levant and Europeans, such as the Dutch and the French, in their trade throughout the Middle and Far East.

It also soon acquired a number of other names, many of them in Arabic. And in the eighteenth century as thalers were gaining a foothold in the countries bordering the Red Sea they were seen and noted by European travellers who referred to them as German crowns, ecus or sovereigns. In the 1760s for example Carsten Niebuhr referred to them as crowns from Austria. German 'crowns' become 'ecus' in French and dollars in English, and with 'dollar' the difficulty is knowing which kind of dollar the writer is referring to – the Spanish or the Austrian. To add to this confusion, the Spanish dollar started life as the real which eventually became the riyal, a currency name common in some Middle Eastern countries.

Above:
Here the Maria Theresa thaler has been turned into a small hinged picture frame.

Opposite right:
Coins of Holy Roman Emperor Francis II (1768-1835) grandson of Maria Theresa who reigned as Emperor Francis I of Austria are to be found in the markets of Arabia where they had a limited circulation in the nineteenth century.

Attempting to trace references to the Maria Theresa thalers in documents of the eighteenth and early nineteenth centuries is not always easy. Much depends on the writer's native tongue, or whether their book is read in translation. The pre-eminent explorers such as Carsten Niebuhr, Sir Richard Burton, Jean Louis Burckhardt, and Gustave Nachtigal give very precise accounts of currency, while others either neglect the subject and some convert monetary terms into their native language. 'Imperial' dollars was the term used by the flamboyant James Bruce of Kinnaird who encountered the Austrian thaler in the course of his journey up the Nile to Ethiopia, with a diversion into Arabia, recorded in his *Travels to Discover the Sources of the Nile* (1790). Bruce also called them *abu taka* or *pataka*. In colloquial Arabic *taka* means window, and it is thought that this refers to the escutcheon on the

reverse of the coin bearing the Habsburg arms which could be said to resemble a window.

When in Zanzibar Sir Richard Burton noted that the Maria Theresa thaler was called *qirsh aswed* (black coin), and the Spanish dollar was known as *qirsh abiyad* (white coin) though he gave no explanation for this distinction. Whilst *qirsh* is a general term for money in Arabic, it can sometimes be used for a specific coin. In Arabia, Burton found that the generic term for dollars was *'riyal fransah'*, a term used to this day in Saudi Arabia, Yemen, Oman and Egypt. The derivation of this term is uncertain, though it might refer to the thalers of the Emperor Francis I, or his grandson Francis II, both of which were circulating in the Yemen, and possibly other parts of Arabia at the end of the eighteenth century. It is most likely that *fransah* and *farangi* are loan words, which have a generic meaning in Arabic for something foreign, and may derive from the time of the Crusader or Frankish incursions into the Levant.

One of the most picturesque names for the Maria Theresa thaler was *abu riysh* (of the feathers) and *abu tair* (of the bird), or simply the bird dollar, which both refer to the double headed Habsburg eagle on the reverse of the coin. Whilst the portrait of the Empress on the face of the coin provides the dominant impression in some countries, and especially in Africa, the reverse of the coin was of greater significance. This is probably because eagles and hawks have a magical significance that goes back to ancient times and feathers – especially those of the ostrich – have long been used as decoration in ritual costume and personal ornament.

Abu shousha was yet another name for the thaler. In Arabic *shousha* means a topknot and this name was probably derived from the image of the young Queen on the thaler where she is portrayed with a bunch of curls on top of her head, though it is also possible that *abu shousha*

refers to the tiara, or even the veil draped down the back of her head.

Riyal Kabir or large riyal was another name in common use in Arabia in allusion to the size of the coin, rather than the size of the Empress, though the French were rather less subtle calling the thaler: *La Grosse Madame.*

In the Sudan the thaler was known as *abu nuqtah* where *nuqtah* refers to the dots or pearls on the brooch, or the tiara, although the pearls on the tiara were shaped more like diamonds. These pearls caused great difficulty over the years for there had to be exactly nine of them to prove the coin was authentic, and if there was one more or less then the coin would be rejected.

In the Amharic language of Ethiopia the thaler was known as *birr*, the word for silver. *Sett birr* referred to female coins or 'woman dollar' and these were valued more highly than *wand birr*, the male coin, where male and female refer to the gender of the figure on the coin. This came about because the coins of Joseph II circulated for a time in Ethiopia although they did not enjoy the popularity of those of his mother the Empress. Across the Red Sea the thaler was also known as the *mukha dollar* in reference to the port of Mocha in the Yemen, which also gave its name to the type of coffee cultivated in the highlands of Yemen.

Nowadays long cumbersome names are often reduced to acronyms. The Maria Theresa thaler – or dollar – has not escaped this fate and is customarily abbreviated to the unromantic 'MTT' or 'MTD'.

IX

HIDDEN HOARDS

*H*e has saved and saved his whole life long and gradually amassed a considerable treasure in the subterranean vaults beneath his palace consisting of shining Maria Theresa thalers dated 1751.

Hans Helfritz on the Imam Yahya of the Yemen, in
The Yemen, A Secret Journey (1958)

Hoards of buried treasure are the stuff of legend, such as the silver stored beneath the statue of the Goddess Athena in the Parthenon that provided the wealth of fifth century Athens. Helfritz's tale of the King of Yemen shows him continuing a tradition of storing much of the wealth of his country beneath his palace. If he was secure in the knowledge that his treasury was overflowing with silver, most of it acquired through taxation of his subjects, he was under constant threat from enemies of his rule, and claimed to need his treasure to defend his realm and consolidate his power.

A comparable case is that of Abd al-Aziz Al

Saud (1902-53), King of Saudi Arabia, who, in the early days of his reign, kept the state treasury in his saddle bags, a necessary strategy for a ruler of a largely nomadic people, and thus constantly on the move to consolidate control of his huge desert kingdom.

The kings of Ethiopia were renowned for their great wealth and in *Voyage sur la côte orientale de la mer rouge*, Rochet d'Hericourt described in 1840 how the ruler Sahla Selassie stored hundreds of thousands of Maria Theresa thalers in a natural subterranean passage. This low narrow chamber was packed with 300 pottery jars brimming with thalers and solid silver. Following the custom of his predecessors these had been placed over a furnace until the coins they held had been reduced to a solid mass. As d'Hericourt tells it, this was done so that the resultant silver bullion could be used to mint Selassie's own coinage: 'It was his fervent hope

Left:
A bridal head dress from Transylvania adorned with Maria Theresa thalers and other Austrian coins of a later date.

that he could obtain a minting machine from abroad. Unfortunately, he realized too late that he had no means to carry out this little vanity, and in any case the principal advantage of possessing silver coins was in their mobility. He had to be content with storing his thalers in leather bags suspended from the vaulted ceiling of the cave.'

The hoarding of thalers in the ground seems to have been a widespread practice in Africa and Arabia before the introduction of western banks in the early years of the twentieth century. Leslie Borer, manager of Barclays Bank in Addis Ababa describes how, after the official opening of the bank there in July 1941, Ethiopian clients began to unearth their hoards of Maria Theresa thalers and deposit them with the bank. 'There was no insuperable difficulty in persuading the people for whom the silver Maria Theresa thalers had been the only monetary medium of exchange for centuries, and who were reputed to abhor all paper money, to part with their unwieldy coins by the ton instead of hoarding them, and to be content to lodge them with a British Bank.' However, the physical process of dealing with these hoards proved troublesome, as Borer explained: 'The enormous labour involved in the handling of dollars had been underestimated and the entire staff remained at the office until all hours counting the cash. The bulk of the dollars had come from the ground, where they had been buried for safety; and the process of counting took place in a cloud of dust. After banking hours the cashier worked in a home-made gas mask. The task proved too time consuming for the overworked staff and it was soon decided that the customers should count their dollars themselves and were instructed to place them neatly in piles of twenty each. A receipt was

given after the amount had been checked and after the close of business the levels were compared and the dollars bagged, 500 in each. The MTTs kept arriving at the bank in ever increasing quantities until all the counter and floor space was full of them. There was not enough staff to cope with them, and an order went out that customers would be limited to $10,000 a day, and these would have to be already counted and sorted into piles of 20 and placed in wooden trays which could be piled one on top of the other thereby bringing a measure of order to the chaos. This solution was known as 'cash and carry' and some 200 tons of MTTs were deposited thus, but it did not entirely solve the problem as the piles of coins still had to be checked and bagged and taken to the strongroom. Frequently the bags developed mildew and burst and when finally the coins were transferred to a currency reserve it was discovered that some 2,000 bags had rotted away leaving one million coins to be recounted.'

If hoarding treasure underground was a natural practice in these societies, it was also a response to fluctuations in the price of silver. When this fell, silver thalers simply disappeared from circulation, and in the event great quantities of them that were known to have been circulating in Ethiopia in the nineteenth century were apparently lost beyond recovery. However, some hoards of 'lost' thalers come to light in odd circumstances. François Regoudy, a numismatist of the Paris Mint writes in *Le thaler de Marie Therese, une Grande Voyageur* (Paris 1992), of a hoard of 700 thalers discovered in Algeria as they were about to be smuggled out by gun-running members of the Front Libération Nationale. On studying these coins Regoudy came to the conclusion that because the majority had been

Above:
Sahla Selassie was reported to have received more then 250,000 Maria Theresa thalers annually in taxes, most of which he stored in subterranean passages in a mountain surmounted by a church.

minted in Rome between 1935 and 1937 they must have been originally shipped to Ethiopia in the years of the Italian occupation, and he surmised that their likely route had been from Ethiopia to Algeria via the Sudan, Egypt, and Libya.

During the Gulf War of 1991 nearly a million Yemeni workers in the Kingdom of Saudi Arabia were summarily deported by King Fahad, in retaliation at the support that the Republic of Yemen gave to Saddam Hussein's invasion of Kuwait.

The economic repercussions for the Yemenis were dire. For years the main source of foreign currency earnings in Yemen came from their workers in Saudi Arabia, a source that had suddenly dried up. Their response was to exploit their savings of Maria Theresa thalers. In *Les thalers d'argent*, Phillipe Flandrin tells how each week in the *souqs* of northern Yemen lorries were loaded with sacks of thalers and then driven across the border to the banks and money changers of Jeddah.

X

FORGERIES AND FABRICATIONS

M*any and various have been the devices employed by private and public malefactors for their own profit to extract gold or silver from the currency, either by debasing the coins with alloy, or by reducing their weight.*

F.W. Hirst
Money: gold, silver and paper (1933)

It was often said that it was impossible to counterfeit the Maria Theresa thaler because it was so finely engraved and so intricately designed. The elaborate edge inscription presented an additional challenge to any forger. Producing an exact replica of the coin was a painstaking task and could only be done by an experienced engraver. However, it would have been surprising if attempts had not been made to counterfeit a coin in circulation for so long. In a legal sense it is not possible to call any copy of

the thaler a forgery as it is not in the strictest sense money; its value depended entirely upon the value of its silver content. Therefore, in this context, a forgery is defined as the production of an unofficial coin as though it had been issued by the ostensible stated authority, but struck in debased silver.

As it happens, millions of Maria Theresa thalers were produced in mints around the world in the twentieth century without the permission of the Austrian authorities, and technically these could be considered as counterfeits. But as explained in the chapter 'Rescues and Ransoms' the circumstances in which they were minted were exceptional, and the fact that the thaler was a trade coin and no longer legal tender in Austria after 1858 was a mitigating factor. The Austrians

---

Left:
Girl from the Shukriya tribe in eastern Sudan wearing a necklace of copies of Austrian coins with the image of Emperor Franz Josef.

Above:

Crude brass imitation of a Maria Theresa thaler. The Arabic inscription maʿadin *on the obverse could refer to the fact that it is made of brass rather than silver.*

protested vehemently against these mintings but were unable to stop them, and some 65 million Maria Theresa thalers were struck over half a century in mints in London, Birmingham, Bombay, Paris, Brussels and Utrecht. As these non-Austrian restrikes are virtually indistinguishable from the originals and as their silver content remained unadulterated, they have been accepted all over the world.

Profit is of course the essential motive for counterfeiting, and in order to make forgery of a silver coin profitable it must either have a reduced silver content or be lighter in weight. Silver coins were customarily made up of pure silver plus a percentage of an alloy, usually copper or some other base metal. Adding more alloy is the commonest way of debasing a coin. It can be difficult to detect adulteration visually although, depending on how much alloy has been added, such a coin is likely to appear dull and lacking in lustre. Maria Theresa thalers in such condition are found from time to time though it is very difficult to tell where they originated. Illegal mints in India, for example, were said to have been supplying thalers to markets in Oman late in the twentieth century.

As a rule the Maria Theresa thaler was simply taken on trust. If it looked genuine and was the appropriate weight it was considered acceptable. Testing for the purity of the silver was a complicated process. One method known since antiquity was working with a touchstone, a type of quartz used for testing silver and gold. A coin was swiped against the stone and from the colour of the mark left on the surface of the stone it was possible to determine the silver content. This method was employed in China where many foreign coins were in circulation, all of which came under careful scrutiny by money changers. An alternative method was to make a small cut in a coin, preferably at the edge, and then to let a drop or two of pure nitric acid into the cut. The resultant colour indicated the quality of the coin: the purer the silver, the whiter the result, the greater the alloy the darker the foaming acid. Naturally, this method of testing is less than ideal as it leaves the coin disfigured. Making a notch in a coin was another way of checking whether it was solid metal or coated, and examples of silver-plated Maria Theresa thalers occasionally come to light. The process known as electroplating

entails the creation of a thin veneer of silver with both the obverse and the reverse images of the coin sealed together over a metal core. If this sort of malpractice is carried out skilfully it is very hard to detect for such a coin may look perfectly genuine. A good test in this case is to toss the coin onto a stone floor for a well struck coin will give a sharp, clear ring while a dull thud signifies that it has probably been cast in a mould and is therefore a counterfeit. Among certain tribes in Arabia the quality of a coin was tested by biting it. If it did not taste or feel right between the teeth it was rejected.

The weight of a coin is critical and *schroffs* or money changers use scales to establish its authenticity. If a Maria Theresa thaler did not

Below:
Crude copies of Maria Theresa thalers used in jewellery. They are of very low silver content and made by casting in a sand mould.

weigh exactly 28,0668 grams, there were grounds for suspicion. But of course coins which had been in circulation for a long time became worn and therefore much lighter in weight, and this could result in their being rejected. A common practice with thalers in this condition was to melt them down for bullion.

Crude copies of thalers are found in the Yemen and Oman, usually for use as a component in jewellery. In cases like this, rather than using the traditional method of a striking between two dies, molten metal is poured into a mould that bears the imprint of the existing coin. Coins made in this way are easily recognizable for the design lacks clarity and sharpness, and a careful

Above:

A silversmith from Nizwa in Oman, using the thaler to weigh silver jewellery. The Maria Theresa thaler weighs almost an ounce or 28.0668 grams. It was used in many countries as a standard of weight against which precious metals were weighed and is known as waqiyyah in Arabic.

Right:

A rare silver gunpowder flask from Oman attached to a shoulder sling which is adorned with different types of thalers. They depict pre-1780 Maria Theresa thalers and also those of Francis I and Francis II which look genuine but are in fact cast copies and are slightly smaller in dimension than the originals.

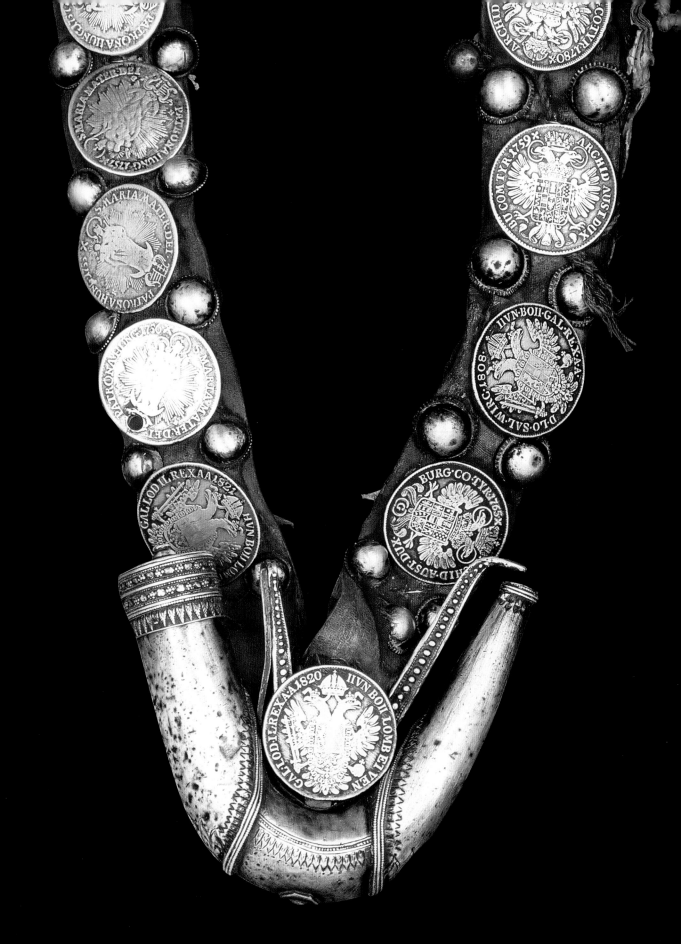

examination usually reveals a surface covered in minute pockmarks. However, not all cast copies are of poor quality. Some of the early Maria Theresa thalers minted in the 1760s were forged in this way and are quite hard to distinguish from the genuine thing. In their book *Oman Adorned,* Miranda Morris and Pauline Shelton argue that the silversmiths of Oman produce very acceptable Maria Theresa thalers by casting them in sand moulds.

Just as today's numismatists study the intricate details of thaler restrikes so the circulation of thalers in Africa and Arabia has long depended upon matters of detail as an index of authenticity. In *Travels in North East Africa 1880-1883* Juan Maria Schuver comments on the kind of scrutiny brought to bear on the details of coins: 'If these stars are more or less effaced or the buckle worn out which secures the mantle of the empress on the shoulder then the Bedouin or camel driver will return you the money as false and without value and even the merchant of the town only accepts it reluctantly.' A preoccupation with the details of the Empress's brooch or her tiara could assume ludicrous proportions. There had to be the exact number of pearls (nine) around the oval brooch, while the coronet should have seven diamonds but sometimes had six or eight. Of course when thalers were scarce there was no option but to accept a coin whatever its condition. At such times transactions would be protracted as each coin was examined at length, and even when coins were accepted it would not be uncommon for the purchaser to return some days later in the hopes of replacing them with more acceptable examples. In Yemen traders would test the authenticity of a coin by feeling for the number of pearls on the brooch.

Major Powell-Cotton, a big game hunter travelling in Ethiopia, reports in his *In Unknown Africa* (London, 1904) that when he paid in Maria Theresa thalers 'Every piece offered is carefully scrutinized, two or three friends being often called in for their opinion. A new one, or one that is much worn or one on which the ornaments on the neck, especially the points of the star, are not clear, is at once rejected. I have had as many as thirty of these coins refused out of fifty, but fortunately no two men agree as to what should be accepted and what not, so that when I reached Asmara there were only some 25 of the 1,500 that no one would look at.' He adds, 'It is however of interest to nobody whether the empress's nose is damaged or her ear shaved.'

This vigilance was simply a way of 'reading the coin' by those unable to interpret the Latin letters or the date on a coin. While we know that variations in the decorative features of coins were made by different mints the silver content was not normally affected by these minor differences. In Oman, Yemen, Sudan and, in particular, in Ethiopia there were incidents of counterfeiting which led to people being suspicious of any slight irregularity. European travellers reported that local people wanted the coin to be 'spick and span' because if it was covered in dirt or dust they suspected that this might hide the fact that it was made of tin. Richard Burton on the other hand reported exactly the reverse: 'No clean money will pass current in this country; all coins must be dirty and gummy otherwise they are rejected; this may be accounted for as the Arabs have no method of detecting false money thus they are afraid to accept any new coin.'

A GOLD FIND

Mystery surrounds the origins of this solid gold Maria Theresa thaler which was purchased recently in a flea market in New Orleans, Louisiana. It came to light some years ago when it was unearthed from among a collection of old cisterns in a long abandoned privy dump in New Orleans. Despite its less than pristine condition the purchaser was thrilled with her find. She had always wanted to own an old coin as it conjured up images of pirates and lost treasure. The surface scratches only made it more interesting and testified to a long and adventurous life. A small part of the lettering was obliterated when it sustained a heavy blow. At one time it was even worn as a belt buckle.

The initials S.F. are missing which points to an unofficial striking. Made from 14-carat gold it weighs 25.9 grams which is much lighter than the small number of gold coins from the Austrian Mint which weigh 51.87 grams. In all other ways however the coin resembles those made from official dies.

One New York collector suggests that this enigmatic coin might have been made in Yemen where thalers of less pure gold were struck and given as gifts to dignitaries and close friends of the rulers in the late 1800s and early 1900s. One London auction house has recently estimated the value of this coin – albeit on the evidence of a photograph and a description – at around US $8,500.

XI

THALERS TRANSFORMED

The situation was made worse by an acute shortage of ready money, for the frivolity of the Bornu people and their partiality for the fair sex converted a considerable part of their Maria Theresa dollars into ornaments, head decorations, and arm and foot bracelets. Many bought goods on credit at excessive prices, to dump them immediately for cash at ridiculously low prices, only in order to procure the silver demanded by their wives and concubines.

Gustave Nachtigal
Sahara and Sudan (1879)

The role played by the thaler in the traditional jewellery and costume of many of the countries of Africa and Arabia was almost as important as its function as currency. The lustrous coin had a profound influence on personal ornamentation both as a component and as a source of silver in jewellery. Imbued with mystical attributes and healing powers, it was admired and worn as decoration by women and sometimes by men from Africa's Atlantic coast to Arabia's eastern shores and beyond. In a corner of the British Museum we find, for example, a handsome ring set with the effigy of the Empress Maria Theresa from Togo in West Africa, while on display in the Bait al Zubair museum in Muscat is a sumptuous wedding necklace called a *marriyah* and lavishly adorned with thalers. Wherever we look in human history it is clear that jewellery and ornament has played an integral part in the lives and customs of men and women, especially in the celebration of events such as birth and

Left:

A bride from Jabal Milhan in the northern Yemen, ritually adorned with traditional wedding ornaments, prominent among them a necklace of Maria Theresa thalers. Jewellery like this was part of the bridewealth and always worn at the special celebrations that marked the various rites of passage.

marriage; occasions when the giving and wearing of jewellery and ornaments seems to transcend the particulars of national and tribal boundaries of time and place. The ceremonial rituals accompanying such events require the inclusion of jewellery as a vital prerequisite, so that a dazzling display of silver or gold wedding jewellery contains a significance beyond the merely decorative.

In *Manners and Customs of the Modern Egyptians* (1890), Edward William Lane wrote that when an Egyptian 'has a sum of money which he does not require for necessary expenses, and cannot profitably employ, he lays it out in the purchase of ornaments for his wife or wives; which ornaments he can easily convert again into money.' In other words, jewellery made from precious metal represented an

Right:
The 'Marriyah', a traditional wedding necklace from Oman which invariably incorporates Maria Theresa thalers.

Below:
The Maria Theresa thaler was an indispensable part of the dowry payment in countries where local coinage was scarce. Seen here are sacks of thalers awaiting distribution to the family of the bride.

important form of family wealth and investment, a commodity that could always be cashed in when the need arose. This is an important aspect in the giving of wedding jewellery and was central to the dowry system. Naturally, dowry customs vary considerably

from country to country. In the Islamic world the custom is for a bride's family to receive a pre-arranged sum of money from a prospective bridegroom as a dowry payment for their daughter, and part of this money would be used to buy jewellery, most commonly made from silver or gold. In Islamic societies this bride-wealth becomes the sole property of the bride, to do with as she likes, and is her source of security for life. It is therefore incumbent on her to acquire as much jewellery as possible at the time of marriage.

Keeping individual wealth in the form of jewellery was a practical solution to the problem of security and acted as a portable bank on which a wife could draw in times of need. Nomadic tribes, who were particularly noted for their robust silver ornaments, would wear their wealth while on the move. For example, the women of the Baggara, a cattle-owning tribe of the western Sudan, wore all their finery while they travelled in search of new pasturage, and were usually accompanied by itinerant silversmiths who melted down and reworked pieces of jewellery when they became too worn.

Wedding regalia was customarily made to order by a silversmith, who might well take up temporary residence with the bride or bridegroom's family whilst working on such a commission. Nomadic or semi-nomadic tribes would employ an itinerant silversmith and larger tribes would probably have their own travelling smiths. The ornaments for these occasions were made in conformity with a long tradition of designs that varied little over the years. Items such as necklaces, headdresses, bracelets, anklets and rings followed the accepted style of marriage jewellery, each country or tribal area having its own specific designs. During protracted

wedding celebrations, which might last several days, a bride was ritually adorned with ornaments, and her feet and hands decorated with henna. The bridegroom also wore ornaments appropriate to the occasion. In Oman the tradition was for a bridal couple to be given Maria Theresa thalers by their guests, who would cast the coins into a wooden bowl before them, though nowadays it is more likely that the coins will be gold. In Yemen, a new husband would traditionally place presents of these coins, together with incense and spices, under his bride's pillow on successive nights. In Sudan and Yemen the custom was for a bride to wear her wedding jewellery for forty days after the wedding whilst she remained secluded in the house of her husband's family, the days enlivened by the company of close female friends.

The religious and symbolic significance of jewellery goes back to the origins of its use, and it has therefore always had an importance beyond its monetary value. At its simplest, personal ornament was derived from a variety of natural substances such as bone, shell and stone which might be worked into beads and bracelets, whilst more valuable materials such as ivory, coral, agate, and amber, would be made into amulets and necklaces. For example amber, a resin fossilised over millions of years, may be found deep in the interior of Africa, transported there from the Baltic shores where it originates. Because gold and silver become liquid and change shape when heated, they have also long been considered magical elements. Gold was likened to the sun, and silver to the moon and both were assumed to have healing properties.

It is generally accepted that the earliest jewellery was worn primarily to protect the wearer, rather than to adorn or beautify. The

Above:
More than 20 silver thalers were melted down to make these traditional anklets from northern Sudan.

body was thought to be vulnerable to malevolent forces or 'the evil eye', which could destroy one's health or psychological well-being, and the wearing of a talisman or amulet was believed to give protection from such forces. A written charm from a holy man or a verse from the Qur'an for example, was held to endow the wearer with immunity from ill-health and other dangers. In *Arabia Felix* (1932), Bertram Thomas tells of his exploration of the Empty Quarter of Arabia during his service as a British political officer and advisor to the Sultan of Muscat in the 1930s. He encountered an old man with two wives who begged Thomas to supply a 'writing' for him. Thomas writes that 'a script worn as a charm is invested with magic virtues. The credulous have no particular concern whether or not it be from the Holy Writ, although it is often a verse from the Koran as the scribe knows no other. Venerated Saiyids do very good business, particularly just before the exodus to the mountains, by vending such. A dollar script will protect against the evil eye; two dollars for an ailing cow; and more for the price of general immunity.'

The amulet case, known as a *hijab* or *hirz* in Arabic, is one of the most popular and widespread forms of jewellery and appears in various shapes and sizes throughout the Middle East and parts of Africa. These phylacteries, or charm cases, are usually made by a silversmith on request, depending on the needs and resources of the customer. The container should be large enough to have a paper inserted and sealed inside. Some, particularly those made of silver, are designed so that they can be opened and re-used. The *hijab* is generally rectangular in shape, or cylindrical with rounded ends, and can be very ornate; the lower edge is sometimes fringed with chains and bells. *Hijabs* do not always contain a written charm and can be purely symbolic, since their shape alone is held to be

Right:
From Oman comes the sumt, *a traditional wedding necklace which includes a number of Maria Theresa thalers which date from the early nineteenth century.*

Below:
A waist belt studded with Maria Theresa thalers from Najran in Saudi Arabia.

enough to give protection. An amuletic writing is only efficacious for the person for whom it is intended and cannot be transferred or borrowed by another. It would provide cover, as it were, for a variety of problems such as physical ailments, psychological difficulties and marital issues. A small silver or leather *hijab* might include a request for help in overcoming an illness, or a woman might order an ornate amulet case in the hope that a charm placed therein would revive

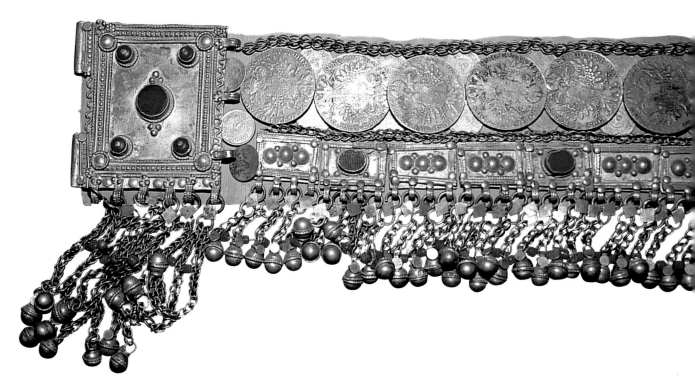

Left:
A conspicuous silver amulet case worn by a woman of the Rashaida tribe in eastern Sudan. It has a hinged opening at one side in order for the written charm or amuletic writing to be replaced if necessary.

the flagging attentions of her husband.

The Maria Theresa thaler was considered to have healing powers when worn on the body, and was believed to be particularly effective at driving away evil spirits or djinns. The 'evil eye' was drawn to the bright shining disc and thereby deflected from the person wearing the thaler. Alternatively, the thaler could be applied directly to the skin or to an infected area to alleviate pain, a practice considered to be a highly effective remedy. King Faisal of Saudi Arabia is said to have used the Maria Theresa thaler in this manner to draw out the toxins from a scorpion sting. Large discs resembling coins were another popular form of amulet. They were hammered out of silver or gold and decorated with geometric designs or with Koranic inscriptions, or sometimes with magic numbers. Known as

hafiydah, which is Arabic for 'protection', these distinctive discs were believed to protect the wearer during childbirth or during circumcision ceremonies. One noted Cairo silversmith reported that his female customers regularly wore the Austrian coin in the belief that it would aid fertility, a conviction related to the common knowledge that Maria Theresa had borne sixteen children.

Traditional African and Arabic jewellery tells one much about its wearer and is usually a reliable indicator of status, rank or tribal affiliations. In some societies a girl may begin to wear a nose ring on marrying, a visible declaration of her new status. To declare their rank, princesses of the Zaghawa tribe of eastern Chad wear ostentatious coral and amber headdresses. Women of the Rashaida tribe in eastern Sudan wear a series of elaborately bejewelled veils which signify the different stages of their lives from puberty to widowhood, while a simple silver cross worn at the neck by many women in Ethiopia signifies their Christian faith.

With the discovery of immense silver deposits in South America in the sixteenth century the metal lost much of its rarity value. Gold jewellery, which confers status and wealth, is popular because it is more easily worked than silver, does not tarnish and retains its value. However, because silver is more robust than gold, it is preferred by nomadic tribes who must always carry their goods and treasure with them, and since it is less expensive than gold, silver ornaments can be made larger and heavier, with more scope for creating interesting and elaborate designs.

Coins of silver and gold, of base metals, and other substances have long been used as components in jewellery, as in the embellishment of costumes and headdresses. For these purposes, thin light coins of low-quality silver or another base metal have always been preferred, for they are easier to pierce and stitch to a dress or headdress. Because such coins were of little intrinsic value they would be used lavishly, especially in Syria, Palestine, Turkey, Egypt and North Africa, where there was a ready supply of small cheap coins. On the other hand, Maria Theresa thalers and Spanish dollars, being of greater value and more imposing, tend to be incorporated into elaborate necklaces or belts. One sometimes comes across thalers that have been gilded or washed in gold, sure evidence that they have been used as a form of jewellery.

In order to suspend a coin in a necklace or about the neck, it needs to have a lug or a ring attached to one edge. In the case of the Maria Theresa thaler this is usually fixed somewhere above the Empress's head, though it is quite possible to come across a thaler where a lug or ring has been fixed at the bottom of the coin, so

Below:
A girl from northern Yemen wears her first necklace comprising thalers worn face inwards and interspersed with beads.

Above:
Silver crosses cut directly from thalers are worn by women in Ethiopia to identify them as Christians. The cross in the middle bears an inscription in Amharic.

Opposite:
As a sign of mourning, this girl from southern Hebron has covered the thalers on her headdress with black cloth. This picture was taken in 1967.

that the Empress is depicted as though standing on her head. The soldering process inevitably causes some disfiguration of the coin, especially where the attachment has been crudely executed. However, these lugs are not only functional objects, but are often ornamental in themselves and transform the thaler into attractive pendants. In Muslim communities the obverse of the coin, with the figure of the Empress, was customarily worn facing inward so as not to offend religious sensibilities by displaying a human effigy. It was more acceptable to show the reverse of the coin facing outwards, for the impressive double-headed Habsburg eagle with its abundance of feathers was a powerful image, and to some eyes more impressive than the portrait of the great Empress herself.

The Arabian peninsula consists of deserts and oases, mountains and fertile lands which have shaped the character and life of its people. It has been a land of passage for trade and pilgrimage, and is scored by ancient incense routes. Camel caravans linked cities like Al-Medinah, Mukalla and Muscat and ancient settlements such as Al-Fau and Marib which are now engulfed in sand. Some of the most distinctive and beautiful silver jewellery in the world has been made in Arabia, worn by both the bedouin and townspeople alike. A good deal of this unique cultural

A Source Of Silver

From the outset of its history, the Maria Theresa thaler was used as a source of silver for jewellery in Africa and the Middle East, inspiring and facilitating a whole genre of personal ornamentation. Today one can still find silversmiths melting thalers down to be reworked into traditional jewellery. According to al-Hamdani, the tenth century Arab geographer, there were ancient sources of silver in Yemen, but there is little evidence that silver was exploited elsewhere in Arabia or in East Africa, where the thaler circulated. India also had to import silver coins in order to satisfy the demand for silver jewellery and the making of silver thread or silver wire for textiles.

Historical accounts of travellers in the nineteenth century document the use of coins in the manufacture of jewellery. Charles Johnston, an English naval surgeon who abandoned his career on the seas to travel overland through Ethiopia in 1840, observed that the women of Shoa were 'exceedingly fond of silver ornaments' and that 'dollars are only valued as the means of thus enabling the possessors to adorn themselves or their women, for all the coin of this sort which enters Shoa ultimately finds its way into the crucible except such as falls into the hands of the King, which are destined for a less useful end, these being securely packed in jars and deposited in caves.'

Melting down and reworking old or damaged silver jewellery was an effective way of recycling silver, particularly in places where precious metals or silver coins were scarce. As a result, silver jewellery seldom reached any very great age. Silversmiths in their workshops, sitting over their anvils were accustomed to seeing their female customers bringing their old ornaments to be transformed. The charge for re-working old silver was usually a percentage of the value of the silver, but there were some silversmiths who were less honest and added to their profit by adulterating the silver with an alloy or by surreptitiously retaining a little of the precious metal.

In the cultures of Africa and Arabia the relationship between a female customer and her silversmith had to be based on trust. Although the silver was weighed, it was never easy to know the exact silver content of a piece, for there was no process for establishing the purity of silver or the quantity of any added alloy, and it is one of the wonders of the silversmiths' craft that they could overcome the difficulties of using varying grades of silver without access to sophisticated assaying equipment. In countries such as Egypt and Libya, silversmiths are required to mark their pieces with a government authorized stamp showing the exact content of silver, but this is not a universal practice. Usually women will sit

Above:
Abib Sa'id, a silversmith from Aleyuh Amba in Ethiopia cutting up a Maria Theresa thaler before melting it down for jewellery. Nineteenth century European travellers to Ethiopia remarked on the large quantities of Maria Theresa thalers that ended up in the crucible: a practice which continues to this day despite the fact that silver can now be cheaply imported from abroad.

Opposite:
A thaler being melted down in a crucible. The picture was taken in the workshop of Abdullah Bahashwan in southern Yemen in 2004.

with the silversmith and watch while their silver is melted down and reworked, paying particular attention to the quantity of silver used in the process. In these communities, silversmiths in the main worked with extremely simple tools, though this does not seem to have inhibited their skills. On the contrary, they produced the most beautiful and intricate pieces stoking their charcoal fire with hand-operated bellows. Nowadays it is likely that a gas blowtorch will have replaced the traditional charcoal fire, and jewellers now work with a hammer and pincers and an anvil set into the ground.

The Maria Theresa thaler is still being used as source of silver, though much silver is now supplied from the Far East. The coin is cut in half before being thrown into the crucible where it is melted at a high temperature. The molten silver is then poured into rectangular moulds and left to cool. The ingot is then hammered out by hand or put through a roller to form a thin sheet of silver. If silver wire is required for filigree work, the sheet is cut into thin strips and pulled by hand through a drawplate. The range of techniques employed by silversmiths over the centuries was remarkable and it is particularly disheartening to see these skills being lost forever as old silversmiths retire without passing on their expertise to sons, who eschew the idea of a long apprenticeship.

heritage has disappeared over the last 50 years. Imported gold jewellery is now much more in fashion, leaving the old silver pieces to be melted down or sold to foreign visitors. In remote enclaves of the peninsula such as the Asir region of Saudi Arabia or the Wahiba Sands of Oman, small tribal groups still wear their opulent jewellery, though as economic developments sweep away the traditional modes of life, such sights as these are becoming less common.

The fame of Yemeni jewellery is well deserved. From the north and south of this fascinating country comes a dazzling array of ornaments, many inlaid with coral or red stones and embellished with swinging chains. The superb workmanship characteristic of Yemeni jewellery was traditionally the work of Jewish silversmiths, but during the middle of the twentieth century many of these skilled artisans left Yemen for the newly-created state of Israel, leaving a void that has gradually been filled by a new generation of indigenous silversmiths.

Silver had to be imported into Yemen, and its use in jewellery was inevitably in competition with the Maria Theresa thaler's use as a currency. As a result, the silver component of Yemeni jewellery was usually heavily alloyed, but what it lacked in the quantity of silver was more than made up for in the intricate workmanship of the silversmiths. There are many regional differences in the forms and designs of Yemeni jewellery, but a universally popular ornament has always been a wedding necklace composed of many strands

Left:
Maria Theresa thalers become dazzling components in a necklace worn by a girl from Jabal Razih in northwestern Yemen, 1977.

of coral beads, with Maria Theresa thalers and a silver *hijab* at its centre. Unlike much silver ornament, such objects become cherished family heirlooms and are carefully preserved from generation to generation.

The sheer diversity of shapes and forms, and the use of filigree and granulation, has made Yemeni jewellery celebrated. Filigree is a technique using drawn silver wire in a decorative manner either on its own or applied to a solid metal base: granulation is a similar technique using different sizes of silver or gold granules which are soldered to a metal base. Both techniques have been in use since ancient times. Large hollow silver beads embellished with filigree and granulation are a feature of northern Yemeni jewellery. Equally popular are their massive silver necklaces worn in multiple layers along with broad chokers, dazzling hair ornaments, multiple earrings, nose-rings and anklets. Conspicuously high-bezelled rings are also typical of Yemen, some in elongated shapes like minarets, others resembling domes and containing scraps of hair, cloth or other relics.

In the cluttered silver shops in the *souq* in Sana'a you will still find a range of fine ornaments for sale, but because of the scarcity of good old pieces, many of the traditional necklaces and belts from the past have been taken apart, segment by segment, to be sold in smaller units, sometimes hung on silver chains. Earrings are also formed in this way using tiny filigree danglers. Yemeni men also wear decorative silver. They seldom go without their *jambiya* or traditional dagger, its ornamental belt hung with various attachments such as a silver powder horn or ammunition box, together with a small knife, a variety of amulet cases and the occasional coin.

On the edge of the Rub' al-Khali, the Empty Quarter, lies the town of Najran, whose market was once a great centre of silver jewellery, much of it imported from Yemen. Today there is little silver left in the *souq*, although Maria Theresa thalers encrusted with coloured stones and bells are still sold as pendants, or may be seen adorning heavy necklaces.

Dir'aah *souq* in the old centre of the sprawling desert city of Riyadh, is a lofty market-place heaped with carpets where the bedouin come in winter to buy their capacious

Opposite:
Coins were a popular embellishment to the traditional costumes of Palestine, Jordan and Syria. Headdresses in particular made use of a variety of coins, including Maria Theresa thalers, seen here adorning the wuqa, *a hair covering, worn by a Palestinian refugee woman in 1970.*

Below:
A typical bridal necklace from Sana'a, composed of coral beads with a silver filigree amulet case. Indian rupees flank a much-worn thaler suspended from the amulet case.

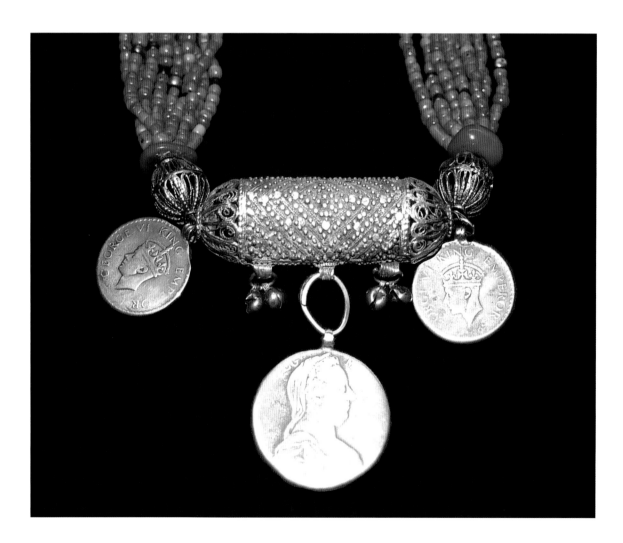

Twenty years ago the bedouin women in the ladies' *souq* in Dir'aah would be found perched among straw mats and loofahs as they presided over the sale of baskets full of spectacular jewellery. Nowadays these colourful vendors have all but disappeared and little of the traditional jewellery survives. The distinctive gold and turquoise ornaments traditional to this region are still on sale but now at prohibitive prices. However, it is still possible to find small supplies of the tenacious *riyal fransah*.

Noted for its elegance, subtlety of form and delicate surface decoration, Omani jewellery is incomparably beautiful. What makes it particularly striking and sets it apart from other jewellery in Arabia is its lustre, the result of using a high-grade silver derived for the most part from Maria Theresa thalers, which impart a special patina. Omani silversmiths have always preferred using silver with as little alloy as possible, and by melting down thalers and extracting most of the small amounts of copper alloy, they manage to produce silver that is close to the 95 per cent purity of sterling silver. Since the Maria Theresa thaler was the official coinage in Oman from the early eighteenth century until the 1970s, it is not surprising that thalers were so often transformed into items of jewellery. One of the most conspicuous examples of this usage is to be seen in the sumptuous bridal necklaces of the interior of Oman, known as *marriyah* and *sumt muttakhal*.

sheepskin cloaks. Here, old men with hennaed beards hawk myrrh and frankincense and indulge in impromptu auctions of battered antiques. For many years Maria Theresa thalers were the primary currency in this part of Arabia, but now these coins lie as exhibits in glass cases, their present value dependant on their age and patina, for the more worn they look the higher the price charged for them. At the kiosk of the official money-changer just down the road from the *souq* neat trays of thalers may be found more moderately priced, and here one Maria Theresa thaler will cost you about £5 sterling.

Omani jewellery is also distinguished by the attention to detail lavished on the individual elements that go to make a whole piece. Hollow silver beads for example, are beautifully proportioned and their endings of exquisitely wrought chains are in the familiar shape of the 'Hand of Fatimah', an icon used throughout Muslim countries as a charm or symbol of good luck or a phylacteric against the 'evil eye.' Silver jewellery from northern Oman has clear stylistic affinities with that of the Indian subcontinent and is distinct from that of the southern region of Dhofar which is more reminiscent of Yemeni silver work.

The Omani *khanjar* or dagger, is the country's national symbol and appears on Omani bank notes. It is is worn at the waist and its shape differs subtly from the ornamental daggers of Yemen and other countries of the Arabian Gulf. More compact and with a smaller hilt than other types of Arab dagger, it has a truncated right angle instead of a sweeping curve at the lower half of the scabbard. The hilt, once made from rhinoceros horn, is now more likely to be made of wood, or even plastic, and embellished with silver. The glory of these daggers lies in their richly-decorated scabbards adorned with filigree or repoussé work, and with chains linked by solid silver rings which in turn are attached to a wide silver-embroidered belt.

The East African countries of the Sudan, Ethiopia, Eritrea and Somalia knew the Maria Theresa thaler as currency from the late eighteenth century and, as in the Arabian peninsula, coveted it as an ornament and as a source of silver for jewellery. Before the opening of the Suez Canal in 1870, thalers were brought in through the Mediterranean port of Alexandria, whence they spread westwards to the north coast of Africa. From Egypt they were transported by boat from Suez down the Red Sea or via the 'forty day road', the caravan route which led from southern Egypt to western Sudan. Although the Austrian coin was accepted as legal tender in Egypt in the nineteenth

Below:

The jambiyah *or* khanjar *is an integral part of the national dress of men in Yemen and Oman, traditionally worn together with an elaborately embroidered belt around the waist. The fine old silver scabbards, which have now become so rare, are objects of great elegance and exquisite workmanship and were wrought from melted-down Maria Theresa thalers. Seen here a* jambiya *of typical Yemeni shape.*

century, it was never the principal currency and circulated concurrently with other European and Turkish coins. According to Mohammed el-Amin, a silversmith who operates a silver business in the Khan al-Khalili bazaar in Cairo, there was a time in the 1950s when Maria Theresa thalers were imported weekly in great numbers – mostly from Yemen – to be used as bullion for jewellery. Amin asserts that rumours of the Empress's legendary fertility had reached the ears of Egyptian women who therefore had a penchant for the thaler's use in amulets, and the coins were also often converted into pendants. And in the villages of the oases of the western desert of Egypt, coin-like discs remain popular as amulets, usually inscribed with magic symbols or Koranic verses.

In the *souq* of Omdurman, across the Nile from Khartoum, nomadic tribes from all over Sudan converge to buy and sell their livestock. During these visits they would take time to order ornaments for their womenfolk from silversmiths, who could be found sitting in the open with their simple tools awaiting commissions. In the past Maria Theresa thalers were a common source of silver, but nowadays the bulk of the silver is imported from China, and here again the contemporary taste is for gold jewellery, which has displaced the traditional popularity of silver pieces. Thus the simple yet elegant silver ornaments that were the mark of much of the jewellery of the Nile Valley are now less in evidence. Characteristic Nile Valley silver jewellery came in crescent-shaped pectorals,

earrings, and nose-rings of beaten silver. Box-shaped amulets with long shivering chains were worn in the hair, and these chains created a delightful percussive rhythm during the performance of tribal dances. Nomadic tribes such as the cattle-owning Baggara or the camel-herding Kababish would employ itinerant silversmiths to make their traditional ornaments, and these were simple and robust pieces made to withstand the rigours of life on the move.

Jewellery and costume in Sudan comes in a rich variety of regional and tribal styles. The Rashaida are a tribe who migrated across the Red Sea from the Hejaz in western Arabia nearly 200 years ago to find new pasturage for their camels. They have prospered in Eritrea and the eastern desert of Sudan, where they live semi-nomadic lives, encamped in black *bait al-sha'ar* (black tents woven from camel wool). Rashaida women decorate themselves in profuse amounts of silver ornaments reminiscent of their Arabian origins: these may include layers of necklaces, spectacular amulet cases, and thalers suspended on silver chains and embellished with semi-precious stones and rows of bells. This profusion of silver can be more often heard rather than seen, for it is customarily concealed beneath elaborate veils worn by Rashaida women from the age of puberty onwards. These are embroidered with silver thread and further embellished with coins and silver trinkets. Rashaida women devote much of their time to acquiring these ornaments from local silversmiths, and follow an almost daily ritual of sitting about in groups dictating to a smith for hours on end, watching his every action, and giving their views in a forthright manner.

In the nineteenth century, the Maria Theresa thaler penetrated westwards to the central regions of Africa where it was used both as jewellery and as a semi-official currency. In the Maghrib and in Libya, the thaler had a more limited circulation, though it turns up not infrequently as decoration on a necklace or a belt. And the women of Mali and Mauritania like to decorate their hair with the thaler , the Spanish dollar, and various French coins.

Historical accounts of nineteenth and twentieth century Ethiopia testify to a widespread use of the Maria Theresa thaler, both as a coin of commerce and as a source of silver for jewellery. In Ethiopia the thaler was referred to as *birr*, the Amharic name for silver, but because *birr* came in time to refer to any kind of dollar coin, the Maria Theresa thaler came to be known as *sett birr*, or 'woman dollar'. Millions of thalers fetched up in the crucibles of silversmiths to be reworked. C.F. Rey recorded his travels in early twentieth century Ethiopia in *Unconquered Abyssinia*, where he writes: 'Silversmiths' work is also to be met with; the manufacture of the highly ornamented trappings of mules and horses used for fantasias and on other gala occasions is fairly general, and so is the making of crosses, rings, earrings and bracelets, head scratchers and ear cleaners, with which the ladies of the country bedeck themselves lavishly. These are mostly made of silver wire, very often gilt, worked in a filigree design and soldered onto silver plates which have been previously hammered out to the shape desired. The silver is obtained by melting down Abyssinian dollars, and the price of the articles is generally fixed at their weight in dollars plus a percentage for workmanship, frequently half as much again.' And Rey makes it clear that 'they – the coins – are wanted not only for purposes of legitimate barter, but are also largely used by the natives for

melting down for making their articles of jewellery and adornment.'

In the centre of Addis Ababa, the modern capital of Ethiopia, lies the *mercato*, a lively marketplace thronged with a proliferation of silversmiths' shops selling a wide variety of ornaments in silver and gold, both traditional and contemporary. Diminutive triangular or semi-circular containers are hung upon dark silk cords, delicate earrings and hair combs shaped with domes and whorls of filigree, phallic-shaped beads and tiny silver trumpets on chains dangle from amulet cases. In this market silversmiths accept commissions as of old from customers and still use the Maria Theresa thaler as a source of silver. In their study of the silversmiths of Ethiopia, Raymond Silverman and Neal Sobania show that the thaler was being used as a source of silver in the town of Harar and elsewhere in Ethiopia as recently as 1993, and thalers remain readily available in the market place and are incorporated into pendants and necklaces.

The ancient city of Axum in Ethiopia has a long tradition of artisans who produce the magnificent ecclesiastical regalia of the Orthodox priests. Large ceremonial crosses made of silver and gold using the lost wax technique are borne aloft during church processions. The lost wax technique is an ancient method of creating metal objects whereby the model is first made in wax then

Left:
These Fulani women from Upper Volta display extravagant hairstyles which they adorn with numerous silver ornaments. Their tresses are weighed down with Maria Theresa thalers.

Right:
The Maria Theresa thaler, if worn prominently, was considered to protect the wearer from the 'evil eye.' Worn here by an Oromo woman from Ethiopia.

covered in a clay mould. This is then heated and the hot wax is poured out through a channel. Molten metal is then poured in to take its place. When the metal has cooled, the mould is broken open to reveal the metal matrix which is then finished by hand. In the past, Ethiopia was well endowed with gold, and wearing jewellery made from this most precious of metals was considered a royal prerogative, although it is now worn by all who can afford it.

Female customers had good reason to be wary in their dealings with silversmiths, given the smiths' common practice of surreptitiously misappropriating silver from the pieces on which they were working on for clients. Mansfield Parkyns, a nineteenth century visitor to Ethiopia, observed in *Life in Abyssinia* that: 'the poor silversmiths here are obliged to be rogues whether they like it or no. I believe they make a tolerably good thing of their business, but it is entirely by appropriating a large portion of both gold and silver entrusted to them for work. The silver they receive is in Maria Theresa thalers: what they return is I should think scarcely so good as a Turkish *piastre* and in fact contains scarcely one half of silver, if so much.'

XII

Rescues and Ransoms

*I*n all our agreements with camel men we have to promise to pay in silver dollars, which is most perplexing as moving up large amounts of silver is very difficult ... our sovereigns command no respect here, whereas great coarse Austrian dollars or Medjidis of doubtful quality are looked upon as real money.

General Garnet Wolseley, Khartoum Relief Expedition 1884

As a coin of such manifest value, the Maria Theresa thaler was destined to become embroiled in a variety of intrigues during its long and eventful career. Ransoms and rewards, skirmishes and smuggling were all part of the history of this popular currency. Bounty was paid in thalers. For example, when Ibrahim Pasha, under orders from the Ottoman Sultan invaded central Arabia in the early nineteenth century, he offered his soldiers five Maria Theresa thalers for every pair of enemy ears

taken during the particularly brutal seven-year-long campaign to bring down the Saudi state.

Blood money was paid in Maria Theresa thalers. The going rate demanded by a murder victim's family in parts of southern Arabia in the mid-1900s was reported to be 700 thalers for a male, and half that amount for a woman. When a British military aeroplane crashed in the remote mountains east of Aden in 1939, the surviving crew were killed by local tribesmen. When their bodies were eventually retrieved by a senior officer and taken by dhow back to Aden, this gruesome cargo included several large sacks of silver thalers given as compensation for the murdered airmen. In a similar incident in August 1949, a Royal Air Force Dakota with a cargo of thalers destined for the payment of troops on the Island of Masirah crashed near Salalah in Oman. All the passengers and crew perished and the cargo of thalers was scattered

---

Left:

The Rashaida, a rich nomadic camel-owning tribe, which emigrated across the Red Sea to the Eastern Sudan in the nineteenth century, are renowned for their copious silver jewellery and elaborately embroidered face masks that they wear from puberty onwards.

over a wide area of the desert to the delight of native tribesmen, who swiftly bore them away. Some time later, during an investigation by the British authorities, the local shaikh insisted that all the thalers should be returned to their rightful owner, in this case the British Government.

Ransom payments, a common feature of life among warring tribal communities in parts of Africa and Arabia, were usually made with a few head of goats or sheep, but for more important captives the offer of silver coinage was considered necessary. When a desperate search for a German explorer missing in Central Africa at the end of the nineteenth century brought no results, a thousand Maria Theresa thalers were offered by the governors of the provinces of Khartoum and Kordofan for his ransom in the

eventuality of his being detained a prisoner. No one came forward to claim the money.

In the 1950s and '60s, the Sultan of Oman invoked a long-standing treaty with the British government to send reinforcements from the British army in his struggle to suppress a Marxist-inspired insurrection in Dhofar. Desert

134

Intelligence Officers, who were established in various towns in the interior, provided the Sultan's forces with vital information, and by the early 1970s the rebels had been destroyed. Maria Theresa thalers were used in these operations to pay locally-enlisted guards and informers, and to make clandestine payments. During the Egyptian-backed revolutionary movement in southern Yemen in the 1960s, local tribesmen could expect to be paid the munificent sum of seven hundred thalers for recovering a large Egyptian mine, or five hundred for a smaller one. This substantial sum was a necessary temptation to induce anyone to carry out such a dangerous task. British soldiers serving in southern Arabia and Ethiopia in the twentieth century were in the habit of sleeping stretched out on top of tea-chests filled with thalers, or using sacks of them as pillows, and when quantities of thalers had to be transported over roads riddled with unexploded mines, soldiers would commonly perch on top of the bullion chests.

LIEUT. GEN. LORD NAPIER, OF MAGDALA, G.C.B, G.C.S.J.

The Maria Theresa thaler was used to fund the dramatic British military expedition in 1867 to rescue the British Consul and other European nationals who had been taken hostage by the erratic Emperor Theodore of Ethiopia. From his headquarters in Bombay, General Sir Robert (later Lord) Napier stated that 'the object of the expedition was to vindicate the dignity of the British Government by procuring the release of Mr Rassam and his suite, and of Consul Cameron, from the captivity in which they had for a long period been most unjustifiably held.' Napier's meticulously planned campaign entailed the transport of ten thousand British troops from India, together with hundreds of horses, mules, camels and some forty elephants, all of which were to be conveyed across the Indian Ocean to the Red Sea and from there into the highlands of Ethiopia. Special boats had to be built just to convey the elephants.

Theodore of Ethiopia harboured a growing resentment towards the British Consul, who had encouraged the Emperor to make overtures of friendship to Queen Victoria, only to receive no response from her. The Foreign Office in London eventually discovered that the Emperor's letter had been inadvertently shelved without being answered. Theodore's response to this imagined rebuff was to imprison the Consul, together with a handful of missionaries and their families. An envoy, Hormusd Rassam, sent by the British to negotiate their release, had promptly been taken hostage himself. The unpredictable Theodore was given to manic rages alternating with wild generosity, one moment sending his prisoners gifts of hundreds of Maria Theresa thalers and the next putting them in chains.

One of Napier's first tasks was to ensure that his army would be well provisioned once they started their trek into the interior of Ethiopia. In a memorandum written before the expedition he wrote, 'nothing could be more unfortunate than

52 THE ILLUSTRATED LONDON NEWS JULY 18, 1868

another illustration, is the attire of what may perhaps be expressed in our vulgar English language by the words "a swell." From the shield hangs the mane of a lion; the cape is enriched with silver and gold ornaments, and in front is a gold cross with precious stones. The cape is red, covered with bosses and ornaments of silver and silver-gilt. One of the bosses was of a very curious design, with a tree of knowledge and two serpents; the other bosses had crosses upon them. The strangely-shaped scabbard was ornamented with a very beautiful bit of filigree-work stuck on its extreme point.

A dinner in the Abyssinian fashion was given by Mr. Rassam to the officers of the 4th (King's Own) Regiment at Antalo. Thirty or forty guests sat upon carpets in a tent, while at the other end of the tent was a party of natives making a "broundo" feast of raw beef. The dinner was brought in by a procession, which reminded one of a pantomime at the London Theatres. There were large baskets covered with red cloth and filled with a kind of bread used by the richer classes, called "teff," which is of a brown colour, like chocolate, made in cakes about 2 ft. in diameter and ¼ in. in thickness. It is full of holes, and light, like sponge-cake, with an insipid taste, but of a slightly acid flavour. It is sometimes eaten by the natives along with a curried pasty, like chutnee. Among the dishes which followed were some curried soups and stews; but the principal one, which seemed most peculiar to the country, was that of the ribs of beef, the meat of which, being all cut off the bone and gathered into a heap, had been roasted till it was black. It ought to be eaten hot from the fire, being at the same time hot with red pepper. Servants held out ribs of this kind, and some helped themselves by cutting slices off the end of the meat. These ribs were sent out to be re-warmed at the fire. Tedge, or a kind of mead produced from honey, is the liquor of the country. This was drunk in tumblers or mugs; but the manner of the Abyssinians is to imbibe it from small bottles with long necks, some of which are introduced into the picture. The ribs of beef were certainly overdone, black to a cinder, and the only resource left open was the broundo, or raw beef, where one found the other extreme. There was rather a want of some intermediate kind of cookery. There were some hot dishes, of a deep reddish orange, from chilies, used as chutnee. After all the dishes had been tasted by the Europeans, the raw beef made its appearance; a servant held up a long slice of it, and four natives commenced by cutting off slices with large curved knives. Some of them held the meat and raised the cut pieces with their hands, after dipping it into the before-mentioned reddish orange paste; but others seized a corner of the meat with their teeth, and while so holding it cut off the portion with a knife. One of these gentlemen was described by Mr. Rassam as having been a functionary in the Court of Theodore—a sort of Lord Chancellor—and his abilities in the way of making large slices of the raw flesh disappear excited the admiration of all present. He flourished his knife in such a style that they feared for his nose; but luckily that organ was short and snubby, so it escaped. It was a question what he would have done if a bit of the nose had chanced to come off. Would it have gone with the rest of the raw meat? One or two of the Europeans tasted the raw beef; but the fear of tapeworm had a most beneficial effect. The little Prince Dojatch Alamaeo attended, and ate some very small portions of the broundo, but he seemed to prefer the cooked article, which a servant cut in small pieces for him with one of the large knives. If the cuisine was not exactly according to the taste of the European palate, the party was a very genial one, and all were delighted with the dinner as an illustration of Abyssinian manners. The officers of the 4th and the others invited were much obliged to Mr. Rassam for the treat he had given them.

While the Snider rifle has been loudly praised for its influence in the Abyssinian war, a far more important piece of ammunition has been too much forgotten—the Maria Theresa dollar. It was more actively used in the expedition than the Snider, and did far more execution. It smoothed the way, and helped the march from Zulla to Magdala. The Snider bullet is a wonderful invention, and not to be depreciated; but it may miss its mark at times, while the dollar is a shot that never fails; everywhere it goes direct to the heart.

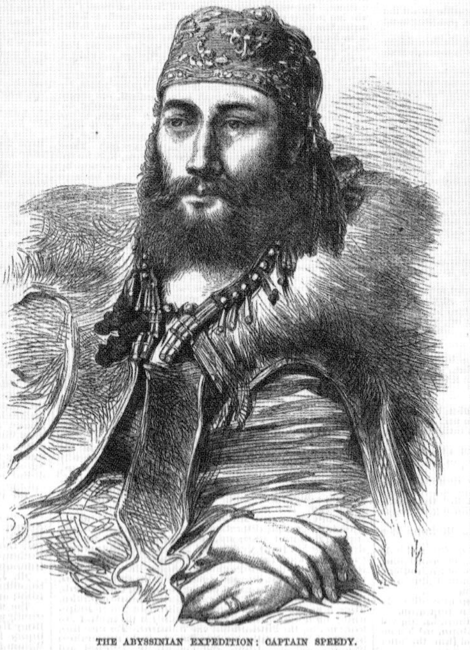

THE ABYSSINIAN EXPEDITION: CAPTAIN SPEEDY.

It is to the very judicious use of this ammunition that a great deal of our success is due in the late campaign. The fire was directed by able hands, and every shot told; so that an ample expenditure of this ammunition has turned out to be the most economical plan in the end. The Maria Theresa dollar seems to have a reputation in many parts of the world, and this it owes to its freedom from alloy. In the reign of that Austrian Empress a number of Spanish galleons had been taken laden with silver from America, and the dollars made from that silver seem to have had a purity that has made them celebrated. Their reputation is so high in Abyssinia that no other coin is current. This was very awkward for Englishmen who wanted to purchase small articles of less value than the dollar, for there was no larger coin and no smaller change. The only small change are the pieces of salt which are carried inland and are used as money. If you wanted to buy a fowl the only plan was to buy as many as you could get for your dollar. If one wanted eggs, there was no coin but the dollar; so one had to get as many eggs or anything else to make up its value. Its real value is equal to about 4s. 3d. The Abyssinians know it under the name of *real*, but its usual name was *coursic*. They also used the word *bir*, or silver, which is with them the equivalent word for money, like the French "argent," the Hindostanee "rupee," and the Scotch "sillar." The Government had learned that this was the only coin that would pass in the country, and they sent large quantities of silver to Vienna to be struck off at the Austrian mint. In monetary transactions with the Abyssinians they were very careful about the inspection of these dollars before accepting them. They had particular marks which they looked out for, and if any of them were wanting the coin was instantly rejected.

We give the portrait of Captain Charles Speedy, who has rendered very important service in the Abyssinian expedition. This gentleman, from 1854 to 1857, served in the 81st Regiment; after which, till 1860, he was Adjutant of the 10th Punjaub Infantry. Having quitted the army he went to Abyssinia; but when he came to Adowa he found that King Theodore would not allow him to leave the country again. He saw the King at Debra Tabor, and was requested to enter his service. But Captain Speedy soon found that it would be improper for a European officer to perform such duties as were required of him, and he never actually did so. Theodore, however, would not allow him to depart; and he accompanied the King, but merely as a spectator, in his war against the Gallas. He received the name of "Basha Fellaka," the first word being the Turkish title of "Pacha," and the other word, "Fellaka," being the Amharic translation of his name "Speedy;" though it also means "glittering," and was applied in this sense to him, because he wore spectacles, which glittered in the sun. Captain Speedy was once threatened with imprisonment at Gaffat, but drew his sword and offered to resist. He was left free, and he then requested permission to leave the country. It was in vain that the King offered him the rank of Lika Makuas (Makuas, he who wears the Royal apparel), or Prime Minister. But this high title was not enough; liberty was preferred, and he was allowed to depart; but previously to leaving, Theodore presented him with a horse and silver trappings and a shield and spear. After this he was for a year Vice-Consul at Massowah, under Consul Cameron. From this Captain Speedy went to New Zealand, and served in the Auckland Militia in Waikato, where he was when he received a telegram from Sir Robert Napier to proceed to Aden, with which he immediately complied, and has been with the Commander-in-Chief during the whole of the expedition. His knowledge of the language and the habits and ideas of the people, and his personal acquaintance of many of the chiefs, have been of the highest value in guiding the decisions and plans of those in command. The finding of supplies on the line of march, particularly near to Magdala, was often entirely due to his knowledge of the country and the feelings of the people in regard to Theodore. On joining the army he, at the request of Sir Robert Napier, adopted the costume of an Abyssinian chief, as it was thought that his constant and important intercourse with the natives might perhaps be facilitated by thus preserving a link of external resemblance, and experience has justified the wisdom of the thought. It is in this costume that we give his portrait, and in it the Captain presents rather a striking figure, for he stands about 6 ft. 6 in. in his stockings. The hirsute portion of the dress which covers the breast and shoulders is a lion's mane, with charms in silver cases attached to it. All Abyssinian chiefs wear a skin of some kind cut into pendants of a similar shape. When our Government approved of the proposal to take charge of Dejatch Alamaeo, Theodore's son, for his education, Sir Robert Napier appointed Captain Speedy, on reaching Zulla, to have the boy under his care, and he has brought him safely to England.

On page 60 is the portrait of another of the notabilities of the Abyssinian expedition—namely, Meer Akbar Ali, a subject of the Nizam of Hyderabad. Meer Akbar Ali, after travelling two years in Syria and Arabia, and visiting the holy places of the Mohammedan religion, conceived the idea of turning his special knowledge and experience to the benefit of the British Government in connection with the late expedition. His application for employment in some honorary capacity was gladly accepted by Sir R. Napier; and his services have proved invaluable at every stage of the expedition in establishing friendly relations between our army and the numerous Mussulman communities of Abyssinia. The special object with which he had been placed on the staff of the expedition remained, however, to be carried out by him on the force approaching Magdala itself. The stronghold of the late King was situated, as is well known, in the territory of a Mohammedan people, called the Wollo Gallas, whom Theodore had made his mortal enemies, but who feared him to such a degree that it was thought probable they would flee before him like sheep whenever he entered their country. To provide, therefore, for such a contingency as the murder of our countrymen by the tyrant, and his subsequent flight from Magdala, Meer Akbar Ali was dispatched from Dalanta to Masteeat, the Queen of the Wollo Gallas, with instructions to cause every outlet by which it was possible for anyone to escape from Magdala to be guarded by her subjects. So well did he succeed in influencing the minds of both the Queen and her people that, during the whole of our operations, Magdala was closely invested by an army of about 8000 Gallas. All these acted under Meer Akbar Ali's orders; and there is no doubt that if King Theodore had fled from the mountain he would immediately have fallen into their hands. The services of this enlightened Mohammedan gentleman are of particular interest, as showing what valuable co-operation it would be possible for us to derive from certain classes of our Indian fellow-subjects if every representative of the British Government in that country were as enlightened as Sir Robert Napier.

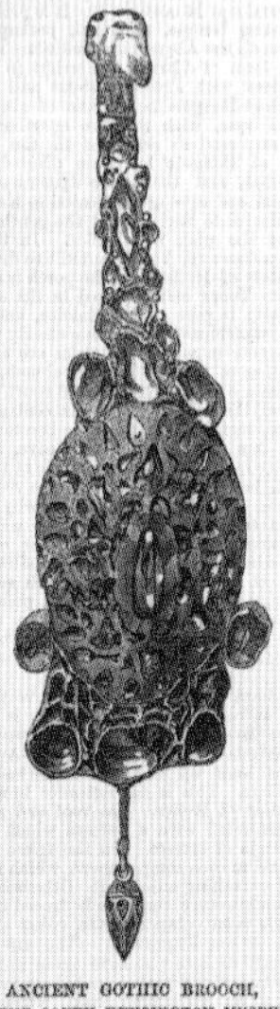

ANCIENT GOTHIC BROOCH,
IN THE SOUTH KENSINGTON MUSEUM.

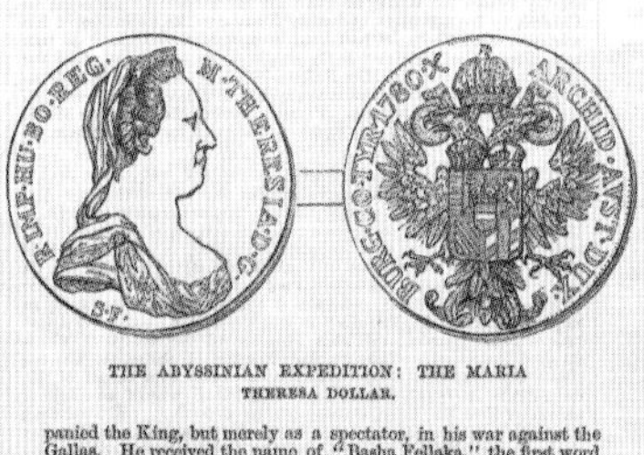

THE ABYSSINIAN EXPEDITION: THE MARIA THERESA DOLLAR.

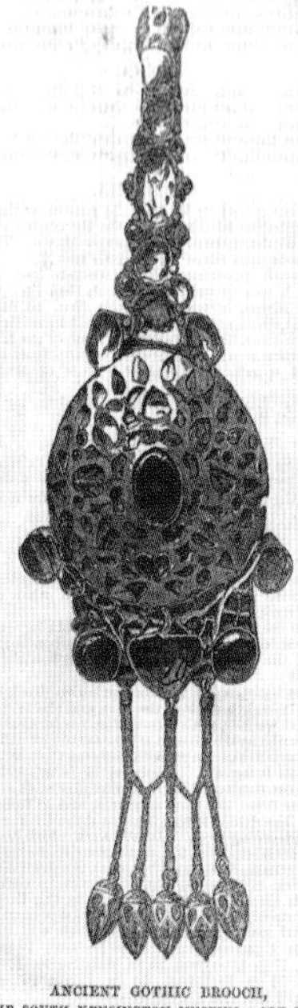

ANCIENT GOTHIC BROOCH,
IN THE SOUTH KENSINGTON MUSEUM.—SEE PAGE 66.

While the Snider rifle has been loudly praised for its influence in the Abyssinian war, a far more important piece of ammunition has been too much forgotten—the Maria Theresa dollar. It was more actively used in the expedition than the Snider, and did far more execution. It smoothed the way, and helped the march from Zulla to Magdala. The Snider bullet is a wonderful invention, and not to be depreciated; but it may miss its mark at times, while the dollar is a shot that never fails; everywhere it goes direct to the heart.

It is to the very judicious use of this ammunition that a great deal of our success is due in the late campaign.

Opposite and above:
From the Illustrated London News, *July 18, 1868.*

---

that the Army should be without money to pay its way ... it appears that we shall need five *lacs* of dollars a month.' (Lac is Hindustani for 100,000 rupees.) A certain Dr Beke, expert in Ethiopian affairs, was consulted. He was adamant that only Maria Theresa thalers would be acceptable in Ethiopia, and that 'any other coin would prove very inconvenient and would lead to considerable financial loss.' There was then a rush to find as many thalers as possible, and agents were sent out to buy up existing stocks wherever they could be found. The Imperial Mint in Vienna was alerted and they offered to coin and deliver any amount of thalers up to 200,000 a week, on condition that the necessary silver was supplied to them. This 'treasure' was shipped out from Trieste and thence via Alexandria to Suez, and on by boat down the Red Sea to the small port of Zeyla. Here the

Above:
The British army marching to Magdala in 1868.

heavy silver coins were checked, counted and re-distributed into wooden crates.

Captain Holland wrote in his official report on the expedition that 'it was found absolutely necessary to have a supply of thalers with the leading columns, so as to pay at once for the supplies tendered and establish a feeling of confidence in the country.' Napier's convoy, many miles in length, had to make its way to Magdala by winding higher and higher up the narrow tortuous paths and defiles of a mountainous region, building bridges across precipitous gorges as it went. At the head of his army rode Napier, accompanied by officers of the Prussian Hussars,

French, Austrian and Spanish cavalry, and scarlet jacketed British troops, their arms glittering and colours unfurled, marching to the music of regimental bands. A vast contingent of camp followers brought up the rear, including the essential animal attendants, *jemadars*, *mahouts*, *duffadars*, *surwans* and *chowdries*, all exotically attired and representing virtually every race and creed from the Indian subcontinent.

Meanwhile, the Emperor waited impatiently in his rocky fortress for the arrival of the British Army. It is said that he thought the soldiers would be female, like their Queen Empress, and was thoroughly put out at the sight of thousands of well-armed men. After an initial bombardment of his stronghold and the deaths of many of his men, he recognized that his chances of any sort of victory were slight. He then attempted to discuss a settlement with Napier, a last desperate act which was met with a rebuff. Unpredictable to the end, he allowed the hostages to leave, and watched as they descended to the British lines below. As the British stormed the fortress, Theodore, rather than be captured, turned his pistol upon himself. Ironically, this had been a gift to him from Queen Victoria in happier times.

Some 20 years later a more famous British military expedition was under way: the rescue of

General Gordon, besieged in Khartoum by the forces of the Mahdi. The commander, General Garnet Wolseley, encountered every sort of difficulty as his army made its way up the Nile. Wolseley wrote that, 'Our sovereigns command no respect here, whereas great coarse Austrian dollars or *Medjidis* of doubtful quality of silver are looked upon as real money. A man who could bring here one hundred thousand pounds in silver would make a good thing of it now in buying up all our sovereigns at a reduced price.' And he continues: 'Silver coinage is so scarce here that it is not easy to have work done in that material. The *Medjidi* & Maria Theresa & Pillar Dollars are really the only coins these people value; of course the Turkish and Egyptian small pieces of a few piastres each excepted. The sovereign is at a great

---

Below:
The elephant train of Armstrong guns and mortars. Forty-four elephants were shipped to Ethiopia, and 39 returned.

discount & few Arabs here will take it. In all our agreements with camel men we have to promise to pay in silver dollars which is most perplexing, as moving up large amounts of silver is very difficult, and even sending as we have done to Constantinople is very difficult to obtain even in Cairo. It takes a long time to make inland people who have little trade with the outside world learn the value of gold coins. Years after our expedition to Abyssinia, men of that country sold handfuls of sovereigns for a few silver dollars.'

The next drama to involve the Maria Theresa thaler came in the 1930s. In his ambition to create a new Roman empire in the Horn of Africa, the Italian dictator Benito Mussolini found it necessary to engage with the thaler, and sought to use it as an economic and political weapon, first by obtaining a monopoly of its production to facilitate his military adventures, and then by suppressing its use in Abyssinia where it was a threat to Italian authority and prestige. After the conclusion of his Abyssinian campaign, Mussolini intended to make the lira the official currency in his conquered territories, and was therefore anxious to stop the import of any further supplies of thalers into Abyssinia. In 1935 the Italian government brought pressure to bear on the Austrians to hand over their dies to the Italian mint, thereby severing the one hundred and 50-year monopoly of the Habsburg mints. To effect this strategy Mussolini's government used the spurious argument that since large parts of modern Italy had been Austrian possessions prior to 1866, it was therefore entitled to mint its own thalers. A view of the British response to this fracture of the Austrian monopoly was given by Sir Robert Johnson, Deputy Master of the Royal Mint, in a minute to the Foreign Office of 13 November,

1935 who wrote: 'It seems that not only are the dollars now being made in Italy, but that the mint at Vienna has received strict instructions not to do anything on their own for anybody else, so that a virtual blockade of the Abyssinian currency is taking place. As a result Italy will be in a strong position to bribe in all parts of the world where these dollars are used, whereas the opposition would be severely handicapped if they can not use bright new dollars when requisitioned. Natives generally view with suspicion any dollars that are at all worn and often will not accept them.' In the event the Austrian mint was compelled to hand over copies of their Maria Theresa thaler dies, and were also forced to limit their own output of thalers to 10,000 annually, and were not permitted to take orders from any other country. Between 1935 and 1937 the mint in Rome struck 18 million thalers.

Italian forces occupied Addis Ababa in 1936 and the Emperor Haile Selassie was forced into exile. While the Italians needed the thaler in the preparation and execution of their invasion, once they had achieved their objective they immediately imposed the Italian lira as the official currency in Abyssinia. At the same time draconian tactics were adopted to outlaw the use of the Maria Theresa thaler, now seen as a threat to Italian authority. They imposed an unrealistic exchange rate of five thalers to one lira, which was totally unacceptable to the native population who were appalled at this attempt to suppress their cherished coin, and they reacted by burying or hoarding thalers in great quantities. As a result the currency situation deteriorated dramatically, and in due course the Italians were forced to acknowledge the thaler as the *de facto* currency in Abyssinia.

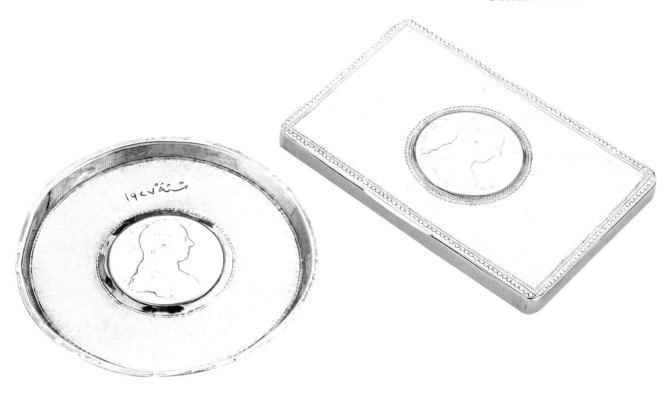

Above:
*Silversmiths frequently used the fashionable
Maria Theresa thaler as a decorative element.
Seen here inset into a handbeaten silver ashtray
and box made in the Sudan in the 1920s.*

When the Italians invaded Abyssinia, some of the principal Fascist leaders, Pietro Badiglio, Rudolfo Graziani and Attilio Teruzzi, used the moment to loot the country. In particular, it is reported that Badoglio appropriated half the 1.7 million Maria Theresa thalers seized by the Italians from the Bank of Ethiopia and used them to build himself a villa in Rome.

Evelyn Waugh covered the invasion of Abyssinia, and wrote in 1936, describing the problem of obtaining thalers: 'The complexity of the situation was impressed on me when I attempted to buy my railway ticket from Diredawa to Addis. I came to the *guichet* with a wallet full of lire and francs. The clerk informed me I must pay in *thalers*. Where was I to get them? With a fine imitation of the classic shrug of the French *"fonctionnaire"* he told me that was my business. I went to Mohammedaly's. The manager told me that his brother had now been waiting ten days, trying to collect enough thalers for his ticket to Djibouti. I was willing to pay a good price for them, I said. So, remarked the manager, was his brother. Mr Costi, the manager of Bololakos's hotel, had a good laugh when I tried to change money with him. Everyone in Diredawa wanted thalers, he said. But what must I do? I must stay in Diredawa like everyone else, Mr Costi suggested ... Eventually a Czecho-Slovak was discovered who had a small cache he was willing to change against sterling; so in great secrecy – we were liable to be gaoled for it – and at an extravagant price, I was able to buy fifty.

The transaction took place in a bedroom. It was like buying cocaine.'

As a result of the Italian conquest the British temporarily lost their Abyssinian market, and with the increased demand for Maria Theresa thalers in adjoining territories such as Sudan and British Somaliland, and in Arabia, they faced problems in safeguarding their long established business interests there. It was against this background that the astute French businessman Antonin Besse was quick to spot that the Maria Theresa thaler offered potential for substantial profits. Besse had built up a trading empire in Aden, and years later was to contribute the funds to found St Antony's College, Oxford. In a letter written in December 1935, he argued that, 'A time is almost certain to come when we shall find it advisable, if not absolutely necessary, to resume our importation from Vienna of MT dollars. A fact which shows which way the wind is blowing is that with silver at about 20d an oz., thus making the dollar work out at Rs (rupees) 1.10, the rate here is notwithstanding maintained at

Rs 1.30, the demand which keeps it so high emanating from Port Sudan, whence the thalers find their way to the Italians in Eritrea, where they are exchanged for lire, which, in their turn, find a ready market in Aden. The profits realized on this traffic are so enormous that the risks it entails – of depreciation of the dollar and being caught – are cheerfully run. Besides the demand for Port Sudan there is a scarcity of thalers in the Hadramut, as well as at Hodeida.' At this point Besse had not realised that Vienna was no longer minting Maria Theresa thalers for foreign customers, and on discovering this to be the case he immediately considered the possibility of having them minted elsewhere. He approached the Royal Mint in London and a meeting was held with London bullion brokers to discuss the possibility of striking thalers in England, and in due course an agreement was reached to do this. The terms of this arrangement required Besse to supply silver bullion to the Royal Mint because silver was scarce in pre-war Britain. There was of course a question of the legality of minting in London a coin that essentially belonged to the Austrians, despite the fact that Vienna could be said to have forfeited its claim to the monopoly of production once it had handed over its minting dies to the Italians. In 1935, Sir Robert Johnson, Deputy Master of the Royal Mint, took legal advice on this matter and was advised that 'as the coin bore a portrait of a 200-year-old monarch of a state that no longer existed and was of a denomination long superseded, the Maria Theresa thalers were simple metallic discs with a design, despite the custom of referring to them as money.' Money or not, these 'metallic disks' were in such demand that London money dealers were vying with each other for a share in their trade and, much against the wishes of the Fascist government in Italy, the Royal Mint prepared its own dies.

Between 1936 and 1941 the Royal Mint struck over fourteen million Maria Theresa thalers. Naturally, other countries soon got wind of this practice, for as Besse had prophesied, it was 'no longer a business, but a fortune falling from the skies', and several European mints began to mint thalers. In 1937 four and half million were minted in Paris, ten million at the Royal Belgian Mint in Brussels, with a small quantity issuing from the mint at Utrecht. Besse was unhappy at this turn of events. In David Footman's biography *Antonin Besse of Aden*, he quotes the following letter from Besse: 'What we would like, would be to make a big profit out of it for ourselves, and smash the market for all these sharks who are speculating in an article which is no concern of theirs whatever.'

The British government's official position was to avoid antagonising the Italians by exporting thalers into Abyssinia once the *de facto* occupation had been recognized, and this remained the case until Mussolini declared war on Britain in June 1940. However a brisk if illicit trade in thalers into Abyssinia continued during the occupation and in October 1937, Signor Grandi, the Italian ambassador in London, protested to Sir Antony Eden, the British Foreign Secretary, that: 'All coining of Maria Theresa dollars by other mints is considered by the Italian Government as improper and performed in violation of the

exclusive right which they possess in virtue of the Anglo-Italian agreement of 9 July 1935, and in these circumstances the Italian Government reserves the right to claim at the proper time and place losses which they may sustain from such improper coining.'

Once Italy had entered the war in 1940 the British government had no further qualms about minting thalers for the support of the Patriot Movement in Ethiopia, and for mounting their counter-attack against the Italians. However, the need to use a cumbersome metal currency presented its own logistical problems. Lord Rennel of Rodd, in his record of the British Military Administration in Africa, argued that: 'The decision to use Maria Theresa thalers was an expensive and onerous one. Minting the coin with its very high silver content, used up the bulk of British silver stocks. For its unitary value, the coin is very heavy; one ton of coin was worth about 3,000 pounds sterling excluding packing.' To alleviate the problems of weight and shipment, use was made of the British mint in Bombay and between 1940 and 1942 the colossal sum of nearly nineteen million thalers was produced in India.

Not all the thirty three million Maria Theresa thalers struck in the Royal Mint and in Bombay were destined for Ethiopia, for a substantial proportion were also distributed in Eritrea, East Africa, Sudan, and Somalia. These consignments were conveyed first by ship and then carried by road in a convoy of lorries with an escort of officers and soldiers over roads that were hardly more than mud tracks.

Glencairn Balfour-Paul, a British officer with the Sudan Defence Force in 1941, who later became the British Ambassador to Baghdad, Jordan, and Tunisia, while in Khartoum was

THE ROYAL MINT

In October, 1935 Sir Robert Johnson, sent a minute to the Foreign Office: 'I should not propose to buy Master Dies from Vienna. We can easily make them here ourselves from specimens of the coin which are in our possession.' He was able to write with such confidence because he was already in contact with a master engraver then living in the Oxfordshire village of Blewbury, whose name was John Langford Jones. An experienced medallist, he was working at the time on a replica of the Emperor Haile Selassie's coin. The Royal Mint sent him a wax enlargement of the Maria Theresa thaler with a request that he make an identical copy, and Johnson urged the utmost haste: 'Please get on with the modelling as fast as possible, particularly if you are anxious to do what you can to save Abyssinia. I need hardly say that, as with the Haile Selassie Dollar, had we had one, it is vital to make an exact imitation in all particulars. You must for instance count the number of small feathers on the wings and copy the minutest details on the Crowns, especially the small ones, otherwise Mr Abyssinia will

Above left:
The Royal Mint had to make their own dies for the Maria Theresa thaler. An electrotype copy was made from an original Maria Theresa thaler.

Above centre:
An English medallist sharpened up the image on a plaster model.

Above right:
The obverse die produced by the Royal Mint.

regard our productions as forgeries (which in fact they are) and refuse to take them. Also, alas, the initials S.F. on the obverse must be repeated and cannot be replaced by your own.' Langford Jones assured him that: 'I hope to produce a fairly competent forgery in reasonable time.' He certainly managed this for in the words of an official of the Mint they 'evolved such perfect copies of the original thalers that they attracted a notable demand from discerning Arab rulers and peoples and led to a useful sideline in the activities of the factory.'

ordered to join a batallion somewhere deep in Ethiopia. The only way he could find of getting beyond Asmara in Eritrea was to cadge a lift on a truck taking bags of thalers to the 'Abyssinian Patriots' a hundred and fifty miles further south. The British sergeant driving the truck gaily told him that: 'If a box or two gets lost when I'm in charge, no one seems to mind.' Sacks of thalers supplied to the battalion that Balfour-Paul joined were intended for the purchase of food for the troops. As Adjutant to the battalion's Commanding Officer, Balfour-Paul was involved in buying whatever supplies other than food that his Colonel deemed necessary. The vagaries of this situation came back to trouble Balfour-Paul in Tripolitania in 1943 when he was still Adjutant to the same colonel. A signal from GHQ Cairo was brought to his tent demanding a full account of their expenditure of thalers in Ethiopia two years earlier. No accounts had been kept, and in great alarm he took the signal to his colonel who said, 'I'll deal with this.' Off went a three-word signal to GHQ: 'Bulls for troops.' No more was heard of the matter.

The Emperor Haile Selassie returned to his capital in 1941 after years in exile, and Barclays Bank opened its first branch in Addis Ababa with a champagne reception. It was a colourful occasion attended by local nobility and several British luminaries including Lord Rennel. The British bank manager, Leslie Borer, described the surge of customers on that first day, as British, South

Left:
Part of a convey of 18 two-ton trucks under armed escort, carrying Maria Theresa thalers from Khartoum to Addis Ababa after its liberation in 1941. At that time £3,000 sterling worth of thalers weighed near to a ton.

Above right:
Maria Theresa thalers being shipped between Port Sudan and Asab.

Below right:
'Paying-in' at the Asmara branch of Barclays bank. The above pictures which give a rare insight into the difficulties of transporting large quantities of Maria Theresa thalers come from the Barclays Bank archives in England.

African, Ethiopian, Greek, Armenian, Indian, Arab, and West African customers entered the bank, including one Tibetan. There was a brisk demand for thalers in exchange for currencies such as East African shillings and Egyptian pounds. However, there were many more customers who wanted to deposit their thalers in the bank and soon hundreds of bags of these coins were piling up behind the counter. Word must have got round that the bank was a reliable repository, and for the first time Ethiopians felt confident about exchanging their thalers for paper money or drafts. Barclays Bank was astute enough to offer advantageous exchange rates.

An announcement appeared in *The Times* of London in 1962 which read: 'No more Maria Theresa coins from London – Vienna regains monopoly. The Royal Mint in accordance with the wishes of the Austrian Government, has discontinued the striking of the Maria Theresa thaler. This ends a somewhat curious chapter of currency history.'

But had England's involvement in this enigmatic coin really ended? On September 12, 1963, the British Prime Minister, Sir Harold Macmillan sent a letter to the Treasury enquiring about Maria Theresa thalers. He wanted to know if they were still being produced in England and if not, when had they ceased being made by the Royal Mint. Finally he wanted to know how difficult it would be and how long it would take to start minting them again. The reasons behind this enquiry remain a mystery but it is more than likely that the Prime Minister was advised that the Austrians had claimed the sole right once again to mint their much admired national icon – the Maria Theresa thaler.

An Answerable Silence –

An interesting sidelight is thrown on the history of the Maria Theresa thaler in the twentieth century through the commercial activities of the London bullion dealers, Johnson Matthey & Co. Ltd., the prime movers in the arrangement whereby the thaler was minted in London during the 1930s. Several European countries whose boundaries were newly demarcated at the end of the First World War began reorganizing their currencies in accordance with the contemporary political situation and prevailing economic conditions. During this period various state banks began to dispose of large quantities of bullion. Johnson Matthey opened a branch in Vienna in 1926 with the intention of buying hoards of demonetised coins, looking for the opportunity to trade internationally in thalers. They quickly monopolized much of this business, and from 1927 orders from all European companies trading in thalers were placed with Johnson Matthey. They not only supervised the dispatch and distribution of coins, but also supplied the bullion for minting them. Huge quantities of silver were involved and in 1927 alone Johnson Matthey supplied bullion for over 12 million thalers made at the Vienna Mint. By 1934, following lengthy negotiations with the Austrian Ministry of Finance, Johnson Matthey succeeded in securing a monopoly over the entire output of thalers from the Austrian Mint, thus effectively securing a monopoly to supply both the silver and the thalers to all those who wished to trade in them, principally, the European banks and merchants trading down the Red Sea. In August 1935 the Austrian Ministry of Finance cancelled this agreement on technical grounds that were legally spurious: an action that was clearly prompted by the Italian Government who had been given the right by the Viennese Mint to strike thalers in Rome. Johnson Matthey now found themselves in a difficult position. The demand for thalers in Africa and Arabia remained substantial and increasing, yet Johnson Matthey was now without the means to supply them. In 1925 Johnson Matthey made enquiries at the Royal Mint in London about the legal implications of the mint manufacturing thalers for their branch in Riga. They pursued these enquiries again in October 1935, and after legal advice, the Mint agreed in 1937 to strike thalers for the company so as to safeguard British influence and trade in Africa and Arabia: an agreement which stipulated that 'distribution to the market be through Messrs Johnson Matthey & Co. Ltd.' On the outbreak of the Second World War in 1939, the British Government took full control of the output of all coinage from the Royal Mint, including thalers. In spite of the fact that the thaler had assumed even greater importance than previously in support of the war effort, Johnson Matthey received no compensation for their loss of business, and in February 1941 they wrote to the Royal Mint in the following terms: 'When the war has been brought to a successful conclusion and the liberation of Abyssinia from the Italian yoke is complete, we shall be interested to know what our thaler position is to be? Is it the intention of the Government to continue its control of the emission of this coinage – which by the way is not a coin at all but a bullion transaction and will involve speculative undertakings – or will it be handed back to us, its rightful owners?'

There is no record of any reply.

JOHNSON MATTHEY & CO. LTD.

TELEGRAMS,"MATTHEY, SMITH, LONDON" ALL CODES USED.   TELEPHONE, HOLBORN 6830/8 (9 LINES).

JOHNSON MATTHEY & CO, LIMITED.

MELTERS & ASSAYERS TO THE
BANK OF ENGLAND.
REFINERS & DEALERS IN
PLATINUM & PRECIOUS METALS.
BULLION MERCHANTS.
SWEEP GRINDERS & SMELTERS.
METALLURGISTS.
ANALYSTS & RESEARCH CHEMISTS.
MANUFACTURING CHEMISTS.
ROLLING & WIRE DRAWING MILLS.
STAMPERS & DIE SINKERS.
CERAMIC PRODUCTS
FOR THE POTTERY, GLASS &
ENAMEL IRON TRADES.

HEAD OFFICES,

73/83, HATTON GARDEN,

London, E.C.1. August 5th 1925.

LONDON
MANCHESTER.
BIRMINGHAM.
BURSLEM.
NEW YORK.
WARSAW.
RIGA.

YOUR REFERENCE

IN YOUR REPLY
PLEASE QUOTE   TG/EP.

> MINT
> RECEIVED
> 6 AUG 1925

The Deputy Master,
H.M.Royal Mint,
LONDON, E. C. 1.

Dear Sir,

        We have been approached by our Riga branch, MM.Silberfeld
Freres, to know whether the Royal Mint would be prepared to manufacture
for us Maria Theresia thalers and other token coinage used in
Abyssinia.

        As far as we are aware the Maria Theresia thaler bear-
ing various eighteenth century dates, is coined by the Austrian Mint
and has been so coined for many years past from the original models
of the thaler.   We believe that they are coined entirely as a commercial proposition, that is to say, to the order of traders with
Abyssinia.

        We are quite ignorant as to the legal aspect of the case
under Austrian law: possibly it is perfectly legal even in Austria
to strike these thalers, working on the analogy that it is legal
in England to strike shillings of the reign of Charles I.   In actual
practice, however, we have no knowledge that these thalers have ever
been coined for Abyssinian merchants except by the Austrian Mint.

        Can you throw any light upon this subject and advise us
how to proceed in the matter ?

        Perhaps you will be so good as to telephone the Writer
regarding this matter as he is anxious to send a cablegram abroad in
connection therewith.

        Yours faithfully,

        For JOHNSON MATTHEY & COMPANY LIMITED.

        Thomas Gorton   DIRECTOR.

Glossary

Agio – the profits made when changing one currency into another.

Alloy – a compound containing a baser metal mixed with a finer.

Blank – a circular disc of metal before it is stamped to make a coin.

Casting – the process of forming a shape by pouring molten metal into a mould.

Collar – a metal ring to hold the blank when a coin is struck.

Cowrie – a small mollusc found in the Indian Ocean which was used as money. Also used as an ornament.

Crucible – a vessel used for melting down metals usually made of earthenware to withstand great heat.

Demonetised – money that has ceased to be legal currency

Die – a stamp, usually made from hard metal that has a design engraved upon it for impressing into some softer material.

Fiat money – money which is made legal tender by government decree.

Fiduciary money – money whose value depends on trust rather than the value of the material from which it is made.

Fine ounce – a troy ounce (480 grains) of pure metal usually gold, silver or platinum.

Haj – Pilgrimage to Mecca.

Hejab, Hirz – An amulet case worn to protect the wearer - Arabic.

Incuse – an impression hammered or stamped in the negative.

Karat – a term which refers to the measurement of gold.

Master punch – a positive engraving with the metal cut away leaving the design up standing. It is used to create coin dies in intaglio.

Matrix – a negative engraving cut by hand or stamped with a master punch.

To mint – to convert bullion into coinage.

Nimsa – Arabic for 'Austria' adj: Nimsawi.

Obverse – the side of a coin chosen as the major side on which the head or principal design is stamped.

Qirsh (pl: qurush) – a coin or money in Arabic.

Reverse – opposite of above.

Restrike – a restrike is a coin or a medal produced with dies which have been decommissioned by their official issuing authority. It can also be a striking done by replicas of the original dies.

Right:
Maria Theresa thalers were a familiar sight in the souq al-Talh in the Yemeni town of S'aada up until the last quarter of the twentieth century.

Bibliography

Annual Report of the Deputy Master and Comptroller of the Royal Mint, HMSO, London 1937, 1939-1944, 1949

Agricola, Georgius, *De re Metallica*, New York 1950

Baker, Sir Samuel White, *The Nile Tributaries of Abyssinia and the sword hunters of the Hamran Arabs*, London 1867

Barclays Bank (DCO), *Quarterly Staff Magazine*, Vol.1, London 1948

Bey, Ali, *Travels of Ali Bey in Morocco, Tripoli, Cyprus, Egypt, Arabia, Syria and Turkey between the Years 1803 and 1807*, London, 1816

Behrens, Robert, 'Maria Theresa's Invisible Empire', *World Coins*, Wisconsin, August 1969

Bent, Mabel, *Southern Arabia*, London, 1900

Broome, M., 'The 1780 Restrike Talers of Maria Theresa', *Numismatic Chronicle*, Vol.XII, London, 1972

Browne, W.G., *Travels in Africa, Egypt and Syria*, London, 1792-1798

Bruce, James, *Travels to Discover the Source of the Nile, 1768-1773*, London, 1804

Burckhardt, Jean Louis, *Travels in Nubia*, London, 1819

————— , *Travels in Arabia*, London, 1829

————— , *Notes on the Bedouins and Wahabys*, London, 1831

Burton, Richard Francis, Sir, *Personal Narrative of a Pilgrimage to Al Madinah and Mecca*, London, 1855-6

————— , *The Lake Regions of Central Africa*, London, 1860

————— , *Zanzibar, City Island & Coast*, London 1872

————— , *First Footsteps in East Africa*, 1894

Chaudhuri, K.N., *Trade in the Indian Ocean*, Cambridge, 1985

Conant, Charles Arthur, *Principles of Money and Banking*, New York, 1905

Cooper, Denis R., *Coins and Minting*, Princess Risborough, 1983

————— , *The Art of Coinmaking*, London, 1988

Crankshaw, Edward, *Maria Theresa*, London, 1969

Cribb, Joe and Barrie Cook, *The Coin Atlas*, London, 1990

Davanzati Bostichi, Bernardo, *Discourse Upon Coins, (1588)*, translated by J. Toland, London, 1696

Davenport, J.S., *European Crowns 1700-1800*, Galesburg, 1961

————— , *The Dollars of Africa, Asia and Oceania*, Galesburg, 1969

Doughty, Charles, *Travels in Arabia Deserta*, London, 1888

Epstein, M., *The Early History of the Levant Company*, London, 1808

Ernst, C., '*Der Levantinerthaler*', *Numismatische Zeitschrift*, 1874

Eypeltauer, T., *Corpus Nummorum Regni Mariae Theresiae*, Basel, 1973

Fischel, Marcel-Maurice, *La Thaler de Marie Thérèse: Etude de Sociologie et d'Historie Economique*, Paris, 1912

Fisher, A., *Africa Adorned*, London, 1984

Flandrin, Phillipe, *Les Thalers d'Argent*, Paris, 1997

Footman, David, *Antonin Besse of Aden*, London, 1986

Forbes, Rosita, *From Red Sea to Blue Nile*, London, 1925

Forrer, Leonard, *Biographical Dictionary of Medallists*, London 1987

Forster, A., *Disappearing Treasures of Oman*, London, 1998

Freeman-Grenville, G.S.P., 'The late Francisco Carbone's Collection of Thalers from Yemen', *Numismatic Chronicle*, London, 1977

Gill, D., *Coinage of Ethiopia and Eritrea*, New York, 1998

Groom, Nigel, *Sheba Revealed*, London, 2002

Hafner, Walter, *Lexicon of the Maria Theresien Taler 1780*, privately printed, Vienna, 1984

Hans, J., *Maria-Theresien-Taler*, Leiden, 1961

Harrigan, P., 'Tales of a Thaler', *Saudi Aramco World*, January/February 2003, pp. 14-23

Hasluck, F.W., 'The Levantine Coinage', *Numismatic Chronicle*, 5th series, London, 1921

Helfritz, Hans, *The Yemen, A Secret Journey*, London, 1958

Herodotus, *The Histories*, (Book 1)

Hirst, F.W., *Money: gold, silver & paper*, London, 1933

Holland, T.J and H. Hozier, *Record of the Expedition to Abyssinia*, HMSO, London, 1870

Ingrao, Charles W., *The Habsburg Monarchy, 1618-1815*, Cambridge, 1994

Johnson, Charles, *Travels in Southern Abyssinia*, London, 1844

Jungwirth, H., 'The Thaler of Maria Theresa and Its Role in International Trade', *One Money for Europe*, Brussels: Belgian Municipal Credit Institution, 1991

Keynes, John Maynard, Review of Fischel in *The Economic Journal*, June, 1914

Krause C.L. and C. Mischler, *Standard Catalogue of World Coins*, Wisconsin, 2000

Lane, Edward William, *Manners and Customs of the Modern Egyptians*, London, 1890

Leypold, F., *Der Marie-Theresien-Taler 1780. (Levantetaler)*, Wiener Neustadt, 1976

Mansur Sheikh (Vincenzo Maurizi), *History of Seyd Said. Sultan of Muscat*, London, 1819

Milburn, W., *The India Trader's Complete Guide*, London, 1825

Miller zu Aicholz, V.von, A.Loehr and E. Holzmair, *Osterreichische Munzpragungen 1519-1938*, Vienna, 1948

Morris, Miranda and Pauline Shelton, *Oman Adorned*, Muscat, 1997

Nachtigal, Gustave, *Sahara and Sudan*, translated by A.G.B. Fisher and H. Fisher, London, 1971

National Archives, Kew, *Records of the Royal Mint.* Class 20: 637/2291/1562/1563

Nebehay, Stefan, 'Kaiserliches Dekolleté und Doppeladler. Zur Erfolgsgeschichte eines monetären', *Markenzeichens Mitteilungen der Anthropologischen Gesellschaft in Wien* 132 (2002) 53-70, Wien

Niebuhr, Carsten, *Travels in Arabia*, Copenhagen, 1772

Pallme, Ignatius, *Travels in Kordofan*, London, 1844

Pankhurst, Richard, 'Economic History of Ethiopia', *Journal of Ethiopian Studies*, Addis Ababa, 1963

——————— ' The Maria Theresa Dollar in Pre-War Ethiopia', *Journal of Ethiopian Studies*, Addis Ababa, 1963

——————— 'The Advent of the Maria Theresa Dollar in Ethiopia, Its Effect on Taxation and Wealth Accumulation, and other Economic, Political and Cultural Implications', *North East African Studies*, 1979-1980

Parkyns, Mansfield, *Life in Abyssinia*, London, 1853

Parsons, Abraham, *Travels in Arabia and Africa*, London, 1808

Peez, C. & J. Raudnitz, *Geschichte des Maria-Theresien-Thalers*, Vienna, 1898

Pope, G., 'The Maria Theresa Dollar in the late Nineteenth and early Twentieth Centuries', *Auf Heller und Cent*, 253-278 Frankfurt –Wien, 2001

Powell-Cotton, Major, *In Unknown Africa*, London, 1904

Raymond, Andre, *Artisans et Commercants au Caire au XVIII siècle*, Institut Français de Damas, Damascus ,1973

Regoudy, François, *Le Thaler de Marie Thérèse 1780, Grand voyageur de temps et de l'espace*, Musée de la Monnaie, Paris, 1992

Rey, Charles F., *Unconquered Abyssinia*, London, 1923

——————— *In The Country of the Blue Nile*, London, 1927

Rochet d'Hericourt, C.F.X., *Voyage sur la côte orientale de la mer Rouge, dans le pays d'Adel et la Royaume de Choa*, Paris, 1841

Rooke, Henry, *Travels to the Coast of Arabia Felix*, London, 1783

Sadleir, George Forster, *A Journey Across Arabia 1819*, Cambridge, 1977

Schienerl, P.W., 'Imitations of European Coins in Sudanese Jewelry', *Ornament* 10(1), California, 1996

Schuver, Juan Maria, *Travels in North East Africa 1880-1883*, London,1996. The Hakluyt Society edited by W. James, G. Baumann and D. Johnson

Scott, Hugh, *In the High Yemen*, London, 1942

Serjeant, R.B., and R. Lewcock, *Sana, An Arabian Islamic City*, London, 1983

Silverman, Raymond and Neal Sobania, 'Silverwork in the Highlands', *Ethiopia: Traditions of Creativity.* Michigan State University Museum, 1998

Smith, Adam, *The Wealth of Nations*, London, 1776

Stokes, J.E., 'Die Nachpragungen des Maria-Theresientalers in englischem Auftrag aus Wien. London, Brussel, Bombay and Birmingham', *Numizmatische Zeitschrift*, 94. 1980

Stark, Freya, *A Winter in Arabia*, London, 1940

——————— *The Southern Gates of Arabia*, London, 1936

Stride, H.G., ' The Maria Theresa Thaler', *Numismatic Chronicle*, 6th series. 1956

Sutherland, C.H.V., *Art in Coinage*, London, 1955

Thesiger, Wilfred, *Arabian Sands*, London, 1959

Thomas, Bertram, *Arabia Felix*, London, 1932

Tschoegl, Adrian E., 'Maria Theresa's Thaler: A Case of International Money' *Eastern Economic Journal*, Vol. 27, No. 4, Fall 2001, USA

Tuscherer, Michel, 'Quelques réflexions sur les monnaies et la circulation monétaire en Egypte et en Mer Rouge au XVl et au début du XVll siècle', *Annales Islamologiques*, 33 institut français d'archéologie orientale.

Waugh, Evelyn, *Waugh in Abyssinia*, London, 1936

Wellstead, J.R., *Journey into Oman*, London, 1837

Weir, Shelagh, *Palestinian Costume*, London, 1989

Wheatcroft, Andrew, *The Habsburgs*, London, 1995

Williams, J., with J. Cribb, and E. Errington, *Money, A History*, British Museum Press, London, 1997

Wolseley, General Garnet, *Khartoum Relief Expedition 1884-1885*, London, 1967

Wood, Howland, *The Coin Collectors Journal*, New York, 1936

Wraxall, Sir William, *Memoirs of the Courts of Berlin, Dresden, Warsaw and Vienna*, London, 1886

Index

This index to *A Silver Legend* includes all names of people and places in the text, as well as a comprehensive listing of themes. A number in italics indicates that the item or name appears in an illustration or map on that page, *c* referring to a coin illustration, *j* to an illustration in which jewellery is the main theme, and *m* to a map. It does not preclude further description in the text on the same page.

Words of non-English origin and titles of books and journals are also printed in italics, as in the text. Place names are usually given in their conventional English form with alternatives from the book (where significantly different) shown in brackets. Country names generally include references also to the people and institutions, thus Turkey includes Turks and Turkish.

X

Y

Z